Ministry of Transport.

THE ORIGINAL
HIGHWAY
CODE

Ministry of Transport.

THE ORIGINAL
HIGHWAY
CODE

**Reproductions of
Highway Code booklets
from the Thirties, Forties and Fifties**

MICHAEL O'MARA BOOKS

First published in Great Britain in 2008 by
Michael O'Mara Books Limited
9 Lion Yard
Tremadoc Road
London SW4 7NQ

Text copyright © Michael O'Mara Books Ltd 2008

A CIP catalogue record for this book is available from the British Library

ISBN 978-1-84317-292-5

1 3 5 7 9 10 8 6 4 2

Designed and typeset by Design 23

Printed and bound in Italy by L.E.G.O.

CONTENTS

THE BIRTH OF
THE HIGHWAY CODE

'A code of good manners to be observed by all courteous and considerate persons' is how the very first *Highway Code*, issued in April 1931, was described by the then Minister of Transport, Herbert Morrison.

The Highway Code emerged from legislation that had been introduced to curb the appalling death toll in traffic accidents on Britain's roads. In 1931 there were only 2.3 million vehicles on Britain's roads, yet 7,000 people were killed in road accidents – almost twenty lives lost every single day. Today there are over 30 million vehicles on the road, yet the annual death toll has fallen to less than 3,500, with the general trend being toward fewer fatalities.

The fact that there are now less than half the number of deaths from road accidents, when there are more than ten times the number of vehicles on the roads is due in no small part to manufacturers making all manner of vehicles safer for drivers, their passengers and pedestrians.

Many of today's innovations in vehicle design have been introduced, of course, to comply with government legislation, the

Front cover of the 1931 *Highway Code*.

appearance of the first motor car on Britain's roads in 1894 having prompted almost immediate government involvement. Prior to that first excursion by a two horsepower Benz, the only horsepower witnessed on British roads had been expended by real horses. The horses were occasionally terrified by steam contraptions of various types until people saw the comparative ease with which a petrol-engined car could be operated. Steam power on the road soon became a thing of the past.

The Red Flag Act

The legacy that steam carriages left behind was a sheaf of regulations such as the infamous Locomotive Act of 1865. Known as the 'Red Flag Act', it originally limited the speed of powered vehicles to just 2 mph in cities, towns or villages and 4 mph elsewhere.

It also required that the vehicle be manned by three

The first London to Brighton car run in 1896, staged to celebrate the repeal of the 'Red Flag Act'.

people and that a pedestrian walk sixty yards ahead carrying a red flag to warn other road users of the vehicle's approach.

In 1895, vehicles weighing less than three tons were exempted from the Red Flag Act and the speed limit was raised to a giddy 14 mph in some areas but it quickly became clear that further regulation of motor vehicles would be required for the safety of all road users.

In January 1896, a Mr Arnold of Kent was the first person to be prosecuted for speeding. He was fined one shilling (five pence) for hurtling through a 2 mph zone at an outrageous 8 mph. Mr Arnold's fine was not too harsh, even when put into context with the average weekly wage for a skilled worker at the time of a little under £2 per week.

By 1899, however, speeding motorists had to be wary. In Brighton, a Mr Jeal was prosecuted for driving at a speed that was deemed wholly inappropriate for the traffic and road conditions. He was fined £3 plus court costs or offered the alternative of three weeks in jail. The police reported that he had been travelling at a shocking 12 mph, the court pronouncing that no one need ever travel through Brighton at more than 4 mph.

The First Pedestrian Killed

In August 1896, forty-four-year-old Bridget Driscoll became the first pedestrian in Britain to be killed by a motor car. She was on her way to a dancing display at Crystal Palace, when she was run over by a Roger-Benz car.

At the inquest into her death, witnesses claimed that Bridget had been startled by the car and froze as it approached at a speed of at least 4 mph, although the twenty-year-old driver was accused of having modified the engine to produce up to 8 mph. An expert proved this to have been impossible.

Under the Motor Car Act of 1903, all vehicles had to be

Piccadilly Circus around 1910, showing how horse-drawn traffic shared London's busy streets with the growing throng of motor vehicles.

officially registered and had to display their registration marks, in the form of licence plates, in a prominent position. The annual registration fee was £1 for a car and 5 shillings for a motorcycle. Around the same time, the driving licence was introduced.

The First Driving Licence

There was no requirement for anyone to sit some form of aptitude test in order to obtain a driving licence. Neither were there any eyesight or medical tests. All you had to do was pay the annual fee of 5 shillings (25 pence) at your local Post Office. The minimum driving age was fourteen for motorcyclists and seventeen for all other vehicles. No driver, whatever his or her age, needed to show any knowledge of either the law pertaining to road users or the newly-introduced road signs.

The Motor Car Act had made provision for local authorities to erect road signs, standardizing the hollow red triangle as a hazard warning, the solid red circle to show something that the road user was prohibited from doing and the hollow white circle to indicate a speed limit. Motoring organizations, notably the AA and RAC, also erected road signs, as did cycling clubs, leading to a confusing proliferation of signs by the roadside.

As motor cars began to be mass-produced they became more reliable, and faster, with a consequent increase in the accident rate. The London Safety First Council (which would develop into the National Safety First Association and later the Royal Society for the Prevention of Accidents) was established in 1916 in response to the marked increase in road accidents due to the reduced level of street lighting

A worker paints the lettering on a road sign being manufactured at the Royal Label Factory in Stratford-on-Avon in the mid-thirties.

during the First World War. Among other initiatives, the council distributed thousands of posters providing 'Hints to Drivers of Horsed and Motor Vehicles, and to Cyclists' that included the ditty:

> *The Rule of the Road is a paradox quite,*
> *In Riding or Driving along,*
> *If you KEEP TO THE LEFT you are sure to be RIGHT.*
> *But if you go RIGHT you are WRONG.*

There was a proliferation of vehicles on Britain's roads in the new, modern age following the end of the First World War, leading to greater competition for road space and, in the case of bus drivers, fierce competition for passengers. During the 1920s, 'bus races' were the cause of many accidents. Drivers from rival companies sped through the streets, even forcing each other off the road, in order to be the first to pick up passengers.

The 1931 Highway Code

As a response to the growing anarchy on the roads, the Road Traffic Act of 1930 gave local authorities powers to regulate bus services, made it against the law not to have your vehicle insured and required the Ministry of Transport to prepare guidance for all road users in the form of the new *Highway Code*.

Perhaps the most remarkable thing about the very first *Highway Code* booklet, was that it carried advertising. The front cover of the booklet bore the Ministry of Transport crest as well as a reference to the Road Traffic Act, making the whole thing look like a miniature government 'white paper' policy document, albeit printed in a dull red. The staid presentation made the advertising look even more incongruous. On the back cover was an advertisement for

11

New automatic traffic lights at Ludgate Circus in London in 1930.

the Motor Union Insurance Company, reflecting the new requirement for all vehicles to carry at least 'Third Party' insurance, while inside there were advertisements for the AA, the RAC, BP and Castrol as well as *The Autocar* and *The Motor Cycle* magazines.

The inclusion of advertising followed the style of a series

The first edition carried advertisements such as this one for the RAC.

of booklets issued by the National Safety First Association. Half a million copies of their first booklet providing a 'Safety Code' for road users were distributed in 1924, while in 1926 two million copies of *Road Sense* were issued free to those applying for their first driving licence and *On The Road* was given to anyone renewing their licence. Between them, the NSFA booklets contained far more information than the first *Highway Code*, the April-May 1930 edition of *On The Road* even listing towns throughout the UK where drivers could expect to come across the new automatic traffic lights.

Despite the fact that the first such traffic lights had been installed in Princes Square in Wolverhampton in 1927, there was no mention of traffic lights at all in the 1931 *Highway Code*. There was, however, sound advice for 'all users of the highway' with special attention paid to 'drivers of motor vehicles' who were told that they should 'Be ready to stop when meeting a flock of sheep or a herd of cattle or a pack of hounds.'

The 1935 Highway Code
The 1935 edition was far more comprehensive than its predecessor although then, as now, contravening *The*

Driving instructor Miss Victoria Worsley coaches a pupil in preparation for his driving test in 1936.

Highway Code did not necessarily mean you were breaking the law. But, as was pointed out on the inside cover, 'A failure on the part of any person to observe any provision of the highway code' could count against them during court proceedings.

Illustrations were included to explain the meanings of various road signs and traffic lights got a mention at last, as did the new 30 mph speed limit in built-up areas. For vehicles capable of carrying less than seven passengers, there was still no speed limit on the open road at all.

To ensure that drivers were in possession of the skills required to handle a modern motor car, in 1935 it became compulsory for every driver to sit a test. Within a year the death toll on Britain's roads had fallen by almost a thousand.

Ministry of Transport

THE
HIGHWAY CODE

Issued by the Minister of Transport with the Authority of Parliament

(WITH SUPPLEMENTARY NOTES)

Crown Copyright Reserved

LONDON
PUBLISHED BY HIS MAJESTY'S STATIONERY OFFICE
Price 1d. Net

This Code is issued with the Authority of Parliament
(Resolutions passed May, 1935)

" A failure on the part of any person to observe any provision of the highway code shall not of itself render that person liable to criminal proceedings of any kind, but any such failure may in any proceedings (whether civil or criminal, and including proceedings for an offence under this Act) be relied upon by any party to the proceedings as tending to establish or to negative any liability which is in question in those proceedings."

[20 & 21 Geo. 5. Ch. 43.]

TABLE OF CONTENTS

I. THE HIGHWAY CODE

FOREWORD

BY

THE MINISTER OF TRANSPORT

This Code is put into your hands in the sincere hope that the study and observance of its provisions will make the roads safer and more convenient for you and all others who use the King's Highway.

Its provisions are a simple summary of the best and widest experience, each one of them written down in the resolute desire to prevent that kind of mistake or thoughtless action which may result in some one's bereavement or suffering.

In every human activity there is a standard of conduct to which in the common interest we are expected to conform. This Code is the standard of conduct for the road.

Respect for the Code and for the spirit underlying it is so much a moral duty that its practice should become a habit and its breach a reproach.

Leslie Hore-Belisha

THE
HIGHWAY CODE

TO ALL USERS OF THE ROAD

(1) All persons have a right to use the road for the purpose of passage.

(2) As the manner in which you use the road affects a large number of others, show care and courtesy at all times and avoid unnecessary noise.

(3) Accidents are inevitable unless due allowance is made for possible errors on the part of others.

(4) Before using the road be sure that your alertness or sense of caution is not affected by alcohol or fatigue. A fraction of a second may make all the difference in avoiding an accident. If you cannot give the necessary concentration you are risking not only your own life but the lives of others.

(5) Keep your dog under proper control whether it is on the road or in a vehicle.

(6) Every person who uses the road should learn thoroughly those rules in the Code which apply to him in particular, and should make himself familiar with those which concern other classes of road users.

(7) Learn the traffic signals used by persons regulating traffic and by drivers of vehicles.

TO DRIVERS OF MOTOR VEHICLES
(including Motor Cyclists)

RULE OF THE ROAD

(8) Keep as near to the left as practicable, unless about to overtake or turn to the right. (This rule does not necessarily apply where there are special traffic arrangements as in one way streets or roundabouts.)

CONTROL OF VEHICLE

(9) Remember that the faster you are travelling, the smaller is the margin of safety should an emergency arise, and the more serious must be the result of an accident.

(10) Always be able to pull up your vehicle well within the distance for which you can see the road to be clear, whether by night or by day.

(11) At night always drive well within the limits of your lights. When your headlights are dipped or extinguished be specially careful. If you are dazzled slow down even to a standstill.

(12) Take special care when it is foggy, when light is bad, or when roads are wet, slippery, or otherwise dangerous.

(13) Go slow in narrow roads or winding lanes, however familiar they may be to you.

DUTIES TOWARDS OTHER ROAD USERS

(14) Do not drive in a spirit of competition with other road users. If another driver shows lack of care or good manners do not attempt any form of retaliation.

(15) Remember that you cannot be certain of the movements of pedestrians. Be ready for children who may run suddenly on to the road and for people who may step from a refuge or footpath. Make allowance for the hesitation of the aged and infirm and for the blind.

(16) Give plenty of room to pedestrians and cyclists, especially in wet weather.

(17) Go slow when passing animals and give them as wide a berth as possible. Stop if necessary or if signalled to do so.

(18) Be prepared to meet pedestrians and led animals coming towards you on your own side of the road.

(19) Take special care when passing a stationary vehicle or any other form of obstruction which prevents a clear view of pedestrians or oncoming traffic.

(20) When the traffic in front of you is held up do not encroach on the off-side of the road and thereby impede other traffic.

(21) Never open the door of a vehicle without first making sure that you will not endanger or inconvenience anyone on the road or footpath, and keep a good look out when getting in or out on the offside.

(22) When the load carried on your vehicle projects behind the vehicle it is helpful to other traffic to mark the end of the projection by means of a white cloth.

CROSS ROADS, CORNERS AND BENDS

(23) Take special care at cross roads, corners and bends.

(24) When turning from one road into another go slow and give way to any pedestrians crossing the roads out of which or into which you are turning.

*(25) Proceed with special care when coming from a minor road into a major road and give way to traffic on the major road. Unless you have a clear view of the major road in both directions, stop just before entering the carriageway of the major road.

OVERTAKING

(26) Overtake only on the right, except when a driver in front has signalled his intention to turn to the right. (This rule does not necessarily apply in one way streets.)

(27) Subject to any local provisions to the contrary, tramcars may be overtaken on either side. Before overtaking a tramcar which is about to stop or is stationary watch carefully to see if passengers are about to board or alight. Go slow or stop as the circumstances require.

(28) Never attempt to overtake if by so doing you are likely to inconvenience or endanger any other road user.

(29) Avoid overtaking at a pedestrian crossing.

* See Notes, p. 21.

(30) Overtake only if you can do so without forcing the person overtaken or approaching traffic to swerve or slacken speed.

(31) Never accelerate when being overtaken.

(32) Never cut out, that is, never turn out from the near-side of the road sharply without giving ample warning and being satisfied that it is safe to do so.

(33) Never overtake at a blind corner or I end, or at or approaching the brow of a steep hill or a hump-backed bridge.

(34) Never overtake at cross roads.

REVERSING

(35) Never turn or reverse your vehicle unless you have satisfied yourself that it is safe to do so. Look out specially for pedestrians and children. It is generally better to go to a side road or entrance, back into it and then come forward into the major road.

TRAFFIC SIGNS AND SIGNALS

*(36) Keep a good look out for all traffic signals, signs and lines. (*See* Appendix.)

(37) Before you stop, or slow down or change direction, give the appropriate signal clearly and in good time. If you use a direction indicator, see that it is returned to neutral as soon as your movement is completed.

(38) When approaching a police constable or other person regulating traffic, and where necessary for his guidance, signal the direction in which you intend to go. (*See* Appendix.) Do not rely on signals to proceed given by unauthorised persons.

FILTRATION

†(39) When you are held up at a road junction by a person regulating traffic, do not turn to the left—that is, filter—unless you are given a definite indication to do so by him. (In some districts there may be an exception to this rule at intersections where

---

* See also Notes, pp. 20–24.   † See Note, p. 20.

traffic is controlled by the police and the carriageway is specially marked to indicate that filtration is permitted.)

OBSTRUCTION

(40) When you stop, draw up close to the side of the road, and do not stop opposite a refuge, road repairs or any other obstacle. Never stop opposite or nearly opposite a standing vehicle if by so doing you are liable to cause inconvenience to the passage of other traffic.

*(41) Never allow your vehicle to remain standing close to a bend or road junction, on or near the brow of a hill or a hump-backed bridge, or in any other dangerous position.

(42) Never leave your vehicle standing in such a position as to obscure any pedestrian crossing or traffic sign.

*(43) Never, if it can be avoided, leave your vehicle facing the wrong way in foggy or misty weather or at night on an unlit or badly lit road.

(44) Never, if it can be avoided, put questions to a constable regulating traffic ; you distract his attention and may cause obstruction or danger.

CONVOYS

(45) If you are a driver in a convoy or a driver of one of a series of large vehicles, such as lorries or motor coaches, do not drive close behind the vehicle in front of you. Leave ample space so that a faster vehicle, after overtaking you, can draw in to the left, if necessary, before overtaking the next vehicle.

*PEDESTRIAN CROSSINGS

(46) Look out for pedestrian crossings and make yourself familiar with the rules relating to them.

LAMPS

(47) Dip your headlights when meeting other vehicles on the road unless there are special circumstances which make it unsafe for you to do so.

---

* See Notes, p. 23.

(48) Switch off or dip your headlights when you are following another vehicle which you do not intend to overtake.

(49) Do not use your headlights unnecessarily, especially in lighted areas.

(50) On foggy days turn on your side and tail lamps.

HORNS AND NOISE

*(51) Make as little noise as you can. Do not sound your horn unnecessarily or race your engine when your vehicle is stationary. Sudden noisy acceleration is unnecessary and disturbing.

(52) Remember that the sounding of your horn does not give you the right of way or absolve you from the duty of taking every precaution to avoid an accident.

BRAKES AND TYRES

†(53) Give regular attention to your brakes and see that they are always efficient.

†(54) Always maintain your tyres in a safe condition and, in the case of pneumatic tyres, see that they are kept constantly at a proper pressure.

TO CYCLISTS

RULE OF THE ROAD

(55) Keep as near to the left as practicable, unless about to overtake or turn to the right. (This rule does not necessarily apply where there are special traffic arrangements as in one way streets or roundabouts.)

CONTROL OF VEHICLE

(56) Always keep a good look-out, especially when riding with dropped handlebars.

(57) Remember that the faster you are travelling, the smaller is the margin of safety should an emergency arise, and the more serious must be the result of an accident.

(58) Always be able to pull up your cycle well within the distance for which you can see the road to be clear whether by night or by day.

---

(59) Take special care when it is foggy, when light is bad, or when roads are wet, slippery or otherwise dangerous.

DUTIES TOWARDS OTHER ROAD USERS

(60) Remember that you cannot be certain of the movements of pedestrians. Be ready for children who may run suddenly on to the road and for people who may step from a refuge or footpath. Make allowance for the hesitation of the aged and infirm and for the blind.

(61) Give plenty of room to pedestrians.

(62) Be prepared to meet pedestrians and led animals coming towards you on your own side of the road.

(63) Take special care when passing a stationary vehicle or any other form of obstruction which prevents a clear view of pedestrians or oncoming traffic.

(64) When the traffic in front of you is held up do not encroach on the off-side of the road and thereby impede other traffic.

(65) Do not attempt to gain a forward position in a traffic block by riding along the narrow spaces between stationary vehicles.

(66) Ride in single file whenever road or traffic conditions require it, and never more than two abreast. Avoid riding between tram lines whenever possible ; there is a danger that your wheels may skid when passing over the tram lines or catch in the central slot.

(67) Keep a straight course and do not wobble about the road.

(68) Never ride close behind fast moving vehicles ; always leave enough space to allow for their slowing down or stopping suddenly.

*(69) Never hold on to another vehicle.

(70) Never carry parcels or other articles which may interfere with your control of your cycle or cause damage to others.

---

* See Notes, p. 24.

CROSS ROADS, CORNERS AND BENDS

(71) Take special care at cross roads, corners and bends.

(72) When turning from one road into another go slow and give way to any pedestrians crossing the roads out of which or into which you are turning.

*(73) Proceed with special care when coming from a minor road into a major road and give way to traffic on the major road. Unless you have a clear view of the major road in both directions, stop just before entering the carriageway of the major road.

OVERTAKING

(74) Overtake only on the right, except when a driver in front has signalled his intention to turn to the right. (This rule does not necessarily apply in one way streets.)

(75) Subject to any local provisions to the contrary, tramcars may be overtaken on either side. Before overtaking a tramcar which is about to stop or is stationary, watch carefully to see if passengers are about to board or alight. Go slow or stop as the circumstances require.

(76) Never attempt to overtake if by so doing you are likely to inconvenience or endanger any other road user.

(77) Avoid overtaking at a pedestrian crossing.

(78) Overtake only if you can do so without forcing the person overtaken or approaching traffic to swerve or slacken speed.

(79) Never cut out, that is, never turn out from the near-side of the road sharply without giving ample warning and being satisfied that it is safe to do so.

(80) Never overtake at a blind corner or bend, or at or approaching the brow of a steep hill or a hump-backed bridge.

(81) Never overtake at cross roads.

---

* See Notes, p. 21.

TRAFFIC SIGNS AND SIGNALS

*(82) Keep a good look out for all traffic signals, signs and lines. (*See* Appendix.)

(83) Before you stop, or slow down or change direction, give the appropriate signal clearly and in good time.

(84) When approaching a police constable or other person regulating traffic, and where necessary for his guidance, signal the direction in which you intend to go. (*See* Appendix.) Do not rely on signals to proceed given by unauthorised persons.

FILTRATION

†(85) When you are held up at a road junction by a person regulating traffic, do not turn to the left—that is, filter—unless you are given a definite indication to do so by him. (In some districts there may be an exception to this rule at intersections where traffic is controlled by the police and the carriageway is specially marked to indicate that filtration is permitted.)

‡PEDESTRIAN CROSSINGS

(86) Look out for pedestrian crossings and make yourself familiar with the rules relating to them.

BRAKES AND TYRES

(87) Give regular attention to your brakes and see that they are always efficient.

(88) Always maintain your tyres in a safe condition.

TO PEDESTRIANS

RULE OF THE ROAD

(89) Never walk along the carriageway where there is a pavement or suitable footpath. If there is no footpath it is generally better to walk on the right of the carriageway so as to face oncoming traffic.

---

* See also Notes, pp. 20–24.   † See Notes, p. 20.
‡ See Notes, p. 23.

(90) On a pavement or footpath do not walk alongside the kerb in the same direction as the nearer stream of traffic.

CROSSING THE ROAD

(91) Never start to cross the road without first looking right, then left, and keep a careful look-out until you are safely across. Be specially careful when the road is slippery and where one-way traffic is in force.

(92) Cross the road at right angles whenever possible.

(93) Take special care if you have to step out from behind or in front of a vehicle or any other form of obstruction which prevents a clear view of the road.

(94) Where there is a pedestrian crossing, subway, or refuge, make use of it.

(95) Remember that moving vehicles require time to slow down or stop, particularly when the road is wet or slippery.

*(96) Unless there are " Cross Now " signals do not rely solely on light signals when you are crossing the road. Pay attention to the movements of traffic, and particularly of turning traffic.

STEPPING OFF THE FOOTPATH

(97) Never step off a footpath on to the road even momentarily without making sure that it is safe to do so.

†PEDESTRIAN CROSSINGS

(98) At controlled crossings, i.e., wherever traffic is controlled by police or signals, cross the road only when the appropriate line of traffic is held up.

(99) Never attempt to cross the road just as the traffic is about to start.

---

* See Notes, p. 20. † See Notes, p. 23.

(100) Never stand in the road at blind corners or other places where you may not be seen by approaching drivers or where you may obscure their line of vision.

TO DRIVERS OF HORSE-DRAWN VEHICLES

(101) Remember you are slow moving and keep well to the left of the road unless about to overtake or turn to the right.

(102) Study carefully rules 15, 18–20, 22–30, 32–34, 36, 38–43, 45, 46, which apply to you as well as to the drivers of motor vehicles.

(103) Before you stop or slow down, or change direction, give the appropriate signal with your hand or whip clearly and in good time. (*See* Appendix.)

(104) Always sit on the offside of your vehicle or in such a position that your signals may be easily seen by other road users.

TO RIDERS AND PERSONS IN CHARGE OF

LED HORSES OR OTHER ANIMALS

(105) When leading an animal always place yourself between it and the traffic and keep the animal to the edge of the road. This rule applies equally whether you are yourself walking or riding. Leave the road as clear as possible for other traffic, and make use of grass and other verges, where these are available.

(106) When acting as a drover and there is some other person with you, send him forward so that traffic approaching from either direction can be warned, especially when near a bend or the brow of a hill or when coming out of a gateway on to a road.

(107) Before you let any animal out of a field or yard on to the road, always make sure that the road is clear.

TRAFFIC SIGNALS THAT EVERY ROAD USER SHOULD KNOW

PART I

SIGNALS TO BE GIVEN BY POLICE CONSTABLES AND OTHERS ENGAGED IN THE REGULATION OF TRAFFIC

THE following signals are those officially recommended and are intended to cover the ordinary situations which arise in traffic control, but other signals may be required for abnormal situations or owing to the peculiar lay-out of particular road junctions.

Drivers should note that once they have been stopped the constable may lower his hand or use it for giving other signals. They should not move on until the constable signals to them to do so.

Signals Nos. 1 to 4 are specially illustrated to show how, in a simple instance, they appear to the drivers for whom they are intended. It makes no difference if, as will often happen, the constable's other arm is engaged in making another signal.

An illustration is also given of " Stop " Signals Nos. 1 and 2 combined. Other signals may also be used in combination such as " Stop " Signal No. 1 or No. 2 and " Proceed " Signal No. 4.

Drivers should be specially careful to distinguish the " Proceed " signal intended for them from those intended for other traffic. This will be shown primarily by the constable looking in their direction.

" Proceed " signals are used not only to bring on vehicles which have been stopped, but also to indicate to approaching vehicles that their way is clear.

No. 1. To STOP a vehicle approaching from his front or from either side, the constable faces squarely towards it and extends his right arm and hand at full length above the right shoulder, with the palm of the hand towards the vehicle.

No. 2. To STOP a vehicle approaching from behind, the constable extends his left arm horizontally from the shoulder, and holds it rigid with the back of the hand towards the vehicle.

"Stop" Signal No. 1
as viewed by the driver for whom it is intended.

"Stop" Signal No. 2
as viewed by the driver for whom it is intended.

Nos. 1 and 2 combined. To STOP vehicles approaching from his front and from behind simultaneously the constable combines Signals Nos. 1 and 2 (above).

Combined "Stop" Signals Nos. 1 and 2

No. 3.   To BRING ON a vehicle from his front, the
constable looks towards the driver and beckons him on
with the right hand and forearm, which should be raised
well above the shoulder.

"Proceed" Signal No. 3
as viewed by the driver for whom it is intended.

No. 4.   To BRING ON vehicles from his right or left,
the constable looks towards the driver for whom the
signal is intended, and beckons him on with the right
(or left) hand and forearm, which should be raised well
above the shoulder.

"Proceed" Signals No. 4
as viewed by the drivers for whom they are intended.

Note that the constable does not turn his body,
because he may be holding up vehicles in front of him
and behind him.

PART II

SIGNALS TO BE GIVEN BY DRIVERS AND CYCLISTS TO INDICATE THEIR OWN INTENTIONS

(These signals give information and not instructions to following traffic.)

Signals by drivers should be given with the arm extended from the side of the vehicle at least as far as the elbow, where mechanical indicators are not used.

(a) *SIGNALS TO OTHER DRIVERS*

No. 1. "I am going to SLOW DOWN, or STOP."

Extend the right arm with the palm of the hand turned downwards, and move the arm slowly up and down, keeping the wrist loose.

No. 1

No. 2. "I am going to TURN to my RIGHT."

Extend the right arm and hand, with the palm turned to the front, and hold them rigid in a horizontal position straight out from the off side of the vehicle.

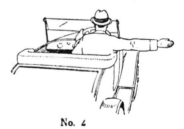

No. 2

No. 3. "I am READY to be OVERTAKEN."

(The overtaking driver must satisfy himself that he can overtake with safety.)

Extend the right arm and hand <u>below</u> the level of the shoulder, and move them backwards and forwards.

No. 3

No. 4. "I am going to TURN to my LEFT."

Extend the right arm and rotate it from the shoulder in an anti-clockwise direction.

No. 4

The drivers of HORSE-DRAWN vehicles should preferably use the four foregoing signals, giving them where possible by hand alone, and in any case keeping the whip (if any) clear of other traffic.

Alternatively, the following signals may be used:—

No. 5. "I am going to STOP."

Raise the whip vertically with the arm extended above the right shoulder.

No. 6. "I am going to TURN."

Rotate the whip above the head; then incline the whip to the right or left to show the direction in which the turn is to be made.

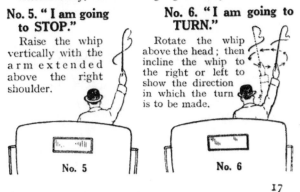

No. 5

No. 6

(b) SIGNALS BY DRIVERS TO POLICE CONSTABLES

When approaching a police constable engaged in the regulation of traffic, drivers of all vehicles should whenever possible indicate to him by means of one of the following signals the direction in which they wish to proceed. The signals are shown in the diagrams as being given with the right hand, but Signals Nos. 7 and 8 may be given with the left hand if more convenient.

No. 7. "I want to GO STRAIGHT AHEAD."

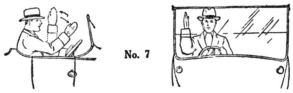

No. 7

Raise the hand towards the shoulder and move the forearm well forwards and then back in a vertical plane, making the movement sufficiently pronounced to be easily seen by the constable.

No. 8. "I want to TURN to my LEFT."

Point the hand to the left, making the movement sufficiently pronounced to be easily seen by the constable.

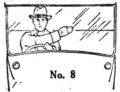

No. 8

No. 9. "I want to TURN to my RIGHT."

Use Signal No. 2.

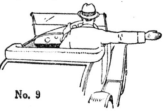

No. 9

SUPPLEMENTARY NOTES

(These notes are merely for the guidance of road users and are not intended to give a complete list of offences under the Road Traffic Acts, 1930-34.)

(i) *DUTY TO STOP AND REPORT ACCIDENTS*

(See Section 22 of the Road Traffic Act, 1930.)

If you are the driver of a motor vehicle which is involved in an accident causing injury to any person, vehicle or animal, you must stop, and if asked to do so, give your name and address, the name and address of the owner of the vehicle and also the identification marks of the vehicle. If for any reason you do not give these particulars at the time of the accident you must report the accident at a police station or to a police constable as soon as possible, and, in any case, within twenty-four hours of its occurrence.

(ii) *THIRD PARTY INSURANCE*

(See Part II of the Road Traffic Act, 1930, as amended by Part II of the Road Traffic Act, 1934.)

If you drive a motor vehicle you must be insured against claims for personal injuries to third parties. If you allow another person to drive your vehicle you must satisfy yourself that your insurance policy or his covers the use of the vehicle while he is driving it.

A certificate of insurance must be obtained from the insurance company and must be produced to a police constable on demand, or, if it is not so produced, it must be produced within five days at a police station specified at the time the certificate is demanded.

If you are the driver of a motor vehicle which is involved in an accident causing injury to another person, you must produce your certificate of insurance at the time of the accident or else produce it at a police station or to a police constable as soon as possible after the accident, and in any case within twenty-four hours.

(a) *To vehicular traffic, including cyclists*

RED	means STOP and wait behind the stop line on the carriageway.
RED AND AMBER ..	means STOP but be prepared to go when the Green shows.
GREEN	means PROCEED if the road is clear but with particular care if the intention is to turn right or left.
AMBER	means STOP at the stop line unless the Amber signal appears when you have already passed the stop line or are so close to it that to pull up might cause an accident.
A GREEN ARROW ..	shown with the RED signal allows vehicles to proceed in the direction indicated by the arrow.

(b) *To pedestrians*

DON'T CROSS ..	means that pedestrians should not cross the carriageway.
CROSS NOW	is a definite invitation to pedestrians to cross the carriageway.

(iv) **DISREGARD OF TRAFFIC SIGNALS** (Rules (36), (39), (82) and (85).)

Under Section 49 of the Road Traffic Act, 1930, it is an offence for any driver or cyclist to disobey the indications given by traffic light signals or by any other traffic sign which regulates the movement of traffic. It is, therefore, an offence under the section to filter, *i.e.*, to turn left against the red signal, unless a green arrow pointing to the left is illuminated at the same time as the red signal.

(v) *ENTERING A MAJOR FROM A MINOR ROAD*

(Rules (25) and (73).)

Under Section 49 of the Road Traffic Act, 1930, it is an offence for any driver or cyclist not to go slow or to come to a stop before entering a major road from a minor road if there is a traffic sign which requires him to do so.

(vi) *TRAFFIC SIGNS* (Rules (36) and (82).)

The following signs are among the more important of the traffic signs, and all road users should be familiar with their significance.

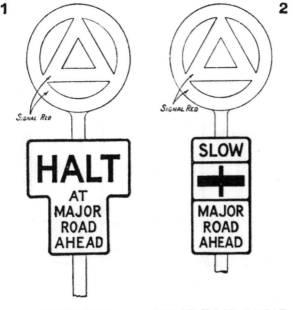

HALT SIGN   **MAJOR ROAD AHEAD**

CROSS ROADS BEND SCHOOL

CROSS
ROADS
3

BEND
4

SCHOOL
5

ROAD JUNCTION

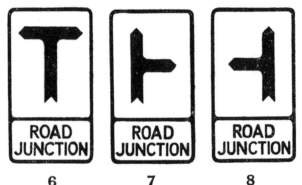

ROAD
JUNCTION
6

ROAD
JUNCTION
7

ROAD
JUNCTION
8

(vii) *LEAVING A VEHICLE IN A DANGEROUS POSITION* (Rules (41) and (43).)

Under Section 50 of the Road Traffic Act, 1930, it is an offence to leave a vehicle on any road in such a position or in such circumstances as to be likely to cause danger to other persons using the road.

(viii) *PEDESTRIAN CROSSINGS* (Rules (46), (86) and (98).)

It is an offence under the Pedestrian Crossing Places Regulations to disobey the following requirements :—

(1) *Drivers of vehicles and cyclists.*

    (*a*) When you are approaching a pedestrian crossing, proceed at a speed which will enable you to stop before reaching the crossing, unless you can see that there is no pedestrian on the crossing.

    (*b*) Where a pedestrian crossing is controlled by police or light signals, allow free passage to any pedestrian who has started to cross before you receive the signal to proceed.

    (*c*) Where a pedestrian crossing is not controlled by police or by light signals, give way to any pedestrian on the crossing.

    (*d*) Never stop on any pedestrian crossing unless you are forced to do so by circumstances beyond your control or to avoid an accident.

(2) *Pedestrians.*

    A pedestrian may not remain on a pedestrian crossing longer than is necessary for the purpose of passing from one side of the road to the other with reasonable despatch.

(ix) *HORNS* (Rule 51).)

It is an offence under the Motor Vehicles (Construction and Use) Regulations, 1934, to sound a horn fitted to a motor vehicle between the hours prescribed by the regulations on any road furnished with a system of street lighting.

(x) *NOISE* (Rule (51).)

It is an offence under the Motor Vehicles (Construction and Use) Regulations not to have an efficient silencer or to use a vehicle in such a way as to cause any excessive noise which could with reasonable care be avoided.

(xi) *BRAKES*   (Rule (53).)

It is an offence under the Motor Vehicles (Construction and Use) Regulations not to maintain brakes on motor vehicles in good and efficient working order or not to keep them properly adjusted.

(xii) *TYRES*   (Rule (54).)

It is an offence under the Motor Vehicles (Construction and Use) Regulations not to maintain the tyres fitted to a motor vehicle in a safe condition.

(xiii) *HOLDING ON TO ANOTHER VEHICLE* (Rule (69).)

It is an offence under Section 29 of the Road Traffic Act, 1930, for a person without lawful authority or reasonable cause to hold on to a motor vehicle or trailer for the purpose of being drawn.

(xiv) *CARRYING A PASSENGER ON A BICYCLE*

Under Section 20 of the Road Traffic Act, 1934, it is an offence for a cyclist to carry a passenger on a bicycle not constructed or adapted for the carriage of more than one person.

(xv) *SPEED LIMIT IN BUILT-UP AREAS*

Under Section 1 of the Road Traffic Act, 1934, it is an offence to exceed a speed of 30 miles per hour on—

    (*a*) a road provided with street lamps, or
    (*b*) a road to which the speed limit has been applied by Order.

At points where the speed limit begins a sign in the following form is used :—

At points where the speed limit ceases a sign in the following form is used :—

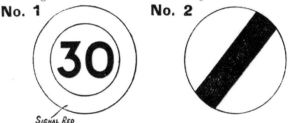

No. 1

Signal Red

No. 2

Certain roads although lit have been freed from the speed limit by Order. In such cases No. 2 signs are fixed to the lamp posts.

LONDON

PUBLISHED BY HIS MAJESTY'S STATIONERY OFFICE

To be purchased directly from H.M. STATIONERY OFFICE at the following addresses:
Adastral House, Kingsway, London, W.C.2; 120 George Street, Edinburgh 2;
York Street, Manchester 1; 1 St. Andrew's Crescent, Cardiff;
80 Chichester Street, Belfast;
or through any Bookseller

Price 1d. Net

88-23

51-6497-5

THE 1946 HIGHWAY CODE

In his foreword to the third edition of *The Highway Code*, Minister of Transport Alfred Barnes urged road users to consider adherence to the principles set out in the code as 'a moral duty' and described road accidents as 'a social evil'.

With the country recovering from six years of war during which more than 450,000 Britons – in uniform and in 'civvy street' – lost their lives, you could be forgiven for thinking that the 'social evil' might have started to look insignificant. In fact, despite fuel rationing and transport restrictions having drastically reduced the overall level of traffic, the number of fatalities rose dramatically during the war.

The main cause of this was the blackout, there being no street lights and all vehicles driving with shielded headlights. Eight thousand people died in traffic accidents during 1939 and by 1941 the total had risen to over nine thousand.

The end of the war in 1945 brought an end to the blackout and, while fuel remained strictly rationed until 1950, an immediate increase in the volume of traffic on our roads. Driving tests, suspended during the war years, were reinstated on 1 November 1946 and the time was ripe for publication of an updated *Highway Code*.

The 1946 *Highway Code* boasted a bold, new design.

Return of the Road Signs

If nothing else, the new *Highway Code* reminded road users what traffic signs looked like. Many signs that had been removed from the roadside during the war in order to confuse and hinder the Germans should they have managed to invade, were now back in place – a welcome return for those who remembered them and a complete novelty for new road users who had never seen them before.

The new front cover design had none of the staid 'parliamentary' look of the first two versions. Instead it was a bold tessellation of images depicting all manner of road users, including horse-drawn carts and a cattle drover alongside modern cars and trucks, a motorcyclist, a cyclist and a couple of jaunty pedestrians.

On page two came the warning that 'Alcohol, even in small amounts, lowers your alertness and sense of caution . . . Many drugs have the same effect . . .' The 1935 edition had advised everyone to 'be sure that your alertness or sense of caution is not affected by alcohol or fatigue' but drinking and driving was clearly of greater concern by 1946.

The general warning given on page two was repeated in different sections of the booklet where motorists were instructed not to 'drive under the influence of a drink or drug'; motorcyclists were advised that the same applied to them; drivers of horse-drawn vehicles were told not to 'drive if you are drunk'; cyclists were warned not to 'ride if you are drunk' and pedestrians were urged never to 'be drunk in any highway or public place'.

The most obvious difference between the 1946 *Highway Code* and its two predecessors was its size. Although it had thirty-two pages as opposed to the second edition's twenty-four, it was not as tall, the actual page size being around twenty per cent smaller. Paper shortages during the years of post-war austerity were almost certainly to blame.

Workmen removing signposts in Surrey during the Second World War to hinder German invaders.

Cyclists Beware!

While the 1946 *Code* included more traffic sign illustrations, the style of the images remained largely similar to that of the 1935 edition. The same was not true of the illustrations used in the section covering 'Signals to be given by Police Constables and others'. The hand and arm signals were identical to those used before but the policeman had lost some of his charm, becoming more of a diagram than the familiar, lovingly-sketched character who had appeared in 1931 and 1935.

The other illustrations in this section were also modernized, giving the third edition a 'forties' rather than a 'thirties' feel, reinforced by the addition of a flat-capped cyclist demonstrating his own hand signals. Cycling was the affordable transport mode of choice for millions in the mid-forties when the Royal Society for the Prevention of Accidents was preparing to launch its Cycling Proficiency Scheme. Before long, over 100,000 people would sit their Cycling Proficiency Test each year.

In the meantime, the *Highway Code* offered some useful advice. In the days when almost every home was heated by open fires and heating in the workplace also generally involved burning coal, soot and smoke in the air combined with fog to produce what we now refer to as 'smog'.

In urban areas this was not only hazardous to your health, but it could also reduce visibility on the road at night to just a few feet. *The Highway Code* warned cyclists riding in fog to 'be prepared to deal with emergencies that would not arise in normal conditions, e.g., finding a vehicle on the wrong side of the road or a pedestrian "lost" on the highway.'

Children learning the rules of the road with miniature signs in a model traffic area in the Lordship Recreation Ground in Tottenham, London.

Safe Stopping Distances

One of the most interesting innovations in the 1946 *Highway Code* was the inclusion of a table of 'stopping distances' for car drivers. These were given as a guide based on ideal road and weather conditions and a vehicle that was performing perfectly.

From 50 mph it was estimated that a competent driver's speed of reaction would give him a 'thinking distance' of 50 feet added to a breaking distance of 125 feet – an overall stopping distance of 175 feet. Amazingly, the 'Typical Stopping Distances' listed in the 2007 edition of *The Highway Code*, although expressed in metres rather than feet, are identical to those published in 1946.

While it could be argued that a modern driver does not react any faster than a driver in the 1940s, therefore the 'thinking distance' should remain the same, modern cars with servo-assisted disc brakes, better tyres, traction control and ABS can stop far more quickly than their 1940s counterparts. Where safety is concerned, no doubt the decision was taken to err on the side of caution and stick with the tried and tested formula first seen in 1946.

STUDY THE FOLLOWING TABLE AND THINK IN TERMS OF OVERALL STOPPING DISTANCE

This is what proper BRAKES can do on good Dry Level Surfaces.

SPEED M.P.H.	THINKING DISTANCE Feet	BRAKING DISTANCE Feet	OVERALL STOPPING DISTANCE Feet
10	10	5	15
20	20	20	40
30	30	45	75
40	40	80	120
50	50	125	175

THINKING DISTANCE = Distance travelled before driver reacts.

BRAKING DISTANCE = Distance travelled after driver applies brakes.

DO YOU REALISE how long it takes to pull up a car in an emergency? This table is based on the assumption that the driver reacts quickly, and that the brakes and road surface are in good condition. The overall stopping distances indicated represent the least margin of safety which can be allowed at different speeds from 10 to 50 miles per hour. Remember that the distances are greatly increased if road or weather conditions are bad or if your vehicle is not in first-class condition. On a skiddy road the braking distances should at least be doubled.

The stopping distances in the 1946 *Highway Code* are the same as those in the 2007 edition.

THE

HIGHWAY

CODE

ISSUED BY THE MINISTER OF TRANSPORT
WITH THE AUTHORITY OF PARLIAMENT
FOR THE GUIDANCE AND SAFETY OF ALL
ROAD USERS

ITH AN APPENDIX
NCLUDING DIAGRAMS
F SIGNALS AND SIGNS

LONDON: PUBLISHED BY
HIS MAJESTY'S STATIONERY OFFICE
ONE PENNY NET

For convenience the Code has been divided into sections, some of which apply specially to certain classes of road users. The following will enable you to see at a glance those sections which more particularly concern you as a—

Foreword

BY

THE MINISTER OF TRANSPORT

In every human activity there is a standard of conduct to which, in the common interest, we are expected to conform. This Code, which is issued with the Authority of Parliament, sets out the standard of conduct for the road.

The provisions of the Code are a simple summary of the best and widest experience. Each provision, whether it relates to a legal requirement or to discretionary behaviour, has been included because of its importance in preventing road accidents.

It is my sincere hope that all road users, whether pedestrians, drivers or riders will study the Code and respect its provisions. To do so is, in fact, a moral duty. If observance of the provisions of the Code, and the spirit of tolerance and consideration underlying them, became a habit, road accidents would rapidly decrease. They are a social evil which can only be overcome by the co-operation of everyone.

Please do not glance at the Code and decide that it does not apply to you : it applies to everyone, and I ask you to study it and act upon it and to encourage others to do so.

THE HIGHWAY CODE

To all Road Users

1   The Highway Code is a set of commonsense provisions for the guidance and safety of all who use
the roads.   Consideration for others as well as for
yourself is the keynote of the Code.   Remember
that you have responsibilities as well as rights.

2   Be careful and courteous yourself at all times;
allow for other people doing something silly at any
minute.

3   Be sure that you are fit to use the road. Alcohol,
even in small amounts, lowers your alertness and
sense of caution. A fraction of a second may make
all the difference between safety and disaster. If you
cannot give the necessary concentration you are risking not only your own life but the lives of others.
Many drugs have the same effect and so also has
fatigue.

4   Learn the signals used for regulating traffic and by
drivers of vehicles. (See pages 14 to 19 inclusive).

The policeman regulating traffic has a responsible 5
job to do. When he is busy don't put questions
to him ; they may distract his attention. If you
want to know the way ask someone else.

Keep your dog under control whether it is on the 6
road or on a vehicle. Many a person has been
killed or injured because a driver swerved to avoid
a dog.

Watch the children. Accidents to small children 7
are terribly frequent.

If you are a parent or guardian teach your own 8
children to cross the road safely and set them an
example by your own road conduct. Do not let
your children play in the streets. Children under
seven should be accompanied by an older person
when using busy roads.

 As a PEDESTRIAN, *study this Section*

GENERAL

Where there is a footpath use it. If there is no 9
footpath it is generally better to walk on the right
so as to face oncoming traffic.

On a footpath do not walk alongside the kerb in 10
the same direction as the nearer stream of traffic.

Do not step off the footpath unless you have made 11
sure that it is safe to do so.

12 Wait until a 'bus or tram has stopped at a recognised stopping place before you get on or off.

13 Do not walk on a cycle track ; leave it free for the cyclists.

14 Never stand in the road at a blind corner or other place where you may not be seen by approaching drivers.

CROSSING THE ROAD

15 Before you cross the road, *stop, look right, left, and right again* ; then cross at right-angles, keeping a careful look-out all the time. Be specially alert on one-way traffic roads.

16 Where there is a pedestrian crossing, refuge, overbridge or subway — use it. (See page 28).

17 If your view of the traffic is obscured by a stationary vehicle or other obstruction, take particular care. If you don't you may be knocked down.

18 A slippery road is dangerous ; watch your step.

19 At traffic signals or at a police-controlled crossing watch the traffic as well as the signals and cross the road only when you can see that it is safe. Look out for traffic turning the corner.

20 Where pedestrian-operated signals are provided, use them, and wait until you see the "Cross now" signal.

21 It is a courteous and kindly act to help small children, the aged, the infirm and the blind to cross the road safely.

If you drive a MOTOR VEHICLE *study this Section and Paragraphs* 41-61.

 If you drive a HORSE-DRAWN VEHICLE *study this Section and Paragraphs* 41-45.

 If you ride a MOTOR CYCLE *study this Section and Paragraphs* 41-43 *and* 46-53.

 If you ride a PEDAL CYCLE *study this Section and Paragraphs* 62-75.

GENERAL

22 Keep well to the left unless you are about to overtake or turn right.

23 When on a narrow winding road, however familiar to you, go slow. You may come upon danger suddenly.

24 Be careful when passing standing vehicles and other obstructions ; a pedestrian may dodge out from behind them.

25 Take special care at cross roads, crossings and bends. If about to turn from one road into another, give the proper signal. When turning, go slow and give way to pedestrians. Give way to traffic on the major road. At uncontrolled crossings, unless you have a clear view of the major road in both directions, stop before entering the major road.

26 When traffic in front of you is held up, never attempt to gain a forward position by encroaching on the offside of the road.

27 Go slow when passing animals and give them plenty of room. Stop if necessary or if signalled to do so. Be prepared to meet pedestrians and led animals coming towards you on your side of the road.

OVERTAKING

28 Never overtake unless you are sure that you can do so without danger to yourself and others. Be specially careful in the dusk when it is more difficult to judge speed and distance.

29 Overtake only on the right except when the driver in front has signalled that he is going to turn right. (This does not necessarily apply at roundabouts and in one-way roads or when overtaking tramcars.)

30 Do not overtake :—

(a) unless you can do so without forcing the overtaken or approaching vehicles to swerve or reduce speed ;

(b) at a corner or bend ;

(c) at or approaching the brow of a hill or a hump-back bridge ;

(d) at cross roads ;

(e) at a pedestrian crossing.

31 Never cut out, that is, do not turn from the near side sharply, without giving ample warning and making sure that it is safe to do so.

32 Give way to pedestrians about to get on or off a tramcar.

SIGNALS AND SIGNS

Before you stop or slow down or change direction, **33** give the proper signal and give it in good time.

Keep a sharp look-out for traffic light signals, traffic **34** signs, and lines marked on the highway. (See pages 20 to 22.)

A policeman regulating traffic is there to help you. **35** Do as he directs, and help him in return by letting him see clearly by your signal which way you want to go.

Do not rely on signals to proceed given by un- **36** authorised persons.

PEDESTRIAN CROSSINGS

Look out for pedestrian crossings. Learn and **37** observe the Regulations relating to them. (See page 28).

FILTERING

When you are held up at a road junction by a **38** police officer regulating traffic, or by a traffic light signal, do not turn to the left unless you get a definite signal to do so. (See pages 15 and 22).

LIGHTS

See that your lights are in good order and are **39** properly adjusted.

Always light up in good time. When visibility is **40** poor and particularly on foggy days, put on your lights so that other people can see you.

If you drive a MOTOR VEHICLE *study this Section and Paragraphs 22-40 and 44-61.*

 If you drive a HORSE-DRAWN VEHICLE *study this Section and Paragraphs 22-40 and 44-45.*

 If you ride a MOTOR CYCLE *study this Section and Paragraphs 22-40 and 46-53.*

GENERAL

41 Give pedestrians and pedal cyclists plenty of room. They are very vulnerable. Be ready for children who may run suddenly on to the road, and for people who may step from a refuge or a footpath or

STATIONARY VEHICLES

42 When you stop your vehicle, draw in as close as possible to the side of the road. Never put it where it endangers or obstructs others. (See page 25). Do not leave your vehicle —

(a) near the brow of a hill or a humpback bridge ;

(b) at or close to a bend or road junction ;

(c) where it obscures a pedestrian crossing or traffic sign ;

(d) at or near a 'bus or tram stopping place or school entrance ;

(e) opposite a refuge, road repairs or other obstacle;

(f) opposite another standing vehicle ;

8

(g) facing the "wrong" way at night, or in fog or misty weather, lest your lights mislead oncoming traffic;

If your vehicle will be stationary for more than a **43** few minutes, put it in a parking space.

 If you drive a MOTOR VEHICLE *study this Section and Paragraphs* 22-43 *and* 46-61.

 If you drive a HORSE-DRAWN VEHICLE *study this Section and Paragraphs* 22-43.

PROJECTING LOADS

A load projecting behind your vehicle may be a **44** danger to others. In daytime mark the end with a white cloth or something else which will attract attention. (At night mark the end of the load with a red light.)

TURNING OR REVERSING (BACKING)

Never turn or reverse (back) your vehicle unless **45** you have made sure that it is safe to do so and that you will not endanger other people. Look out specially for pedestrians and children. When turning a motor vehicle round it is generally best to go to a side road or entrance, back into it and then come forward into the major road.

If you drive a MOTOR VEHICLE *study this Section and Paragraphs 22-45 and 54-61.*

 If you ride a MOTOR CYCLE *study this Section and Paragraphs 22-43.*

GENERAL

46 Take a pride in your driving. The good driver knows how stopping distances increase with speed, and drives accordingly ; drives on his engine and not on his brakes ; knows the braking and acceleration of which his vehicle is capable in an emergency ; and always adjusts his speed to the prevailing road and traffic conditions. (See pages 29-30).

47 Do not drive in a spirit of competition with other road users. If another driver shows lack of care or good manners do not retaliate.

48 Make as little noise as possible. Do not drive on the horn. Use your horn only when it is really necessary : its use does not give you the right of way or absolve you from the duty of taking every precaution.

49 The faster you travel, the smaller will be the margin of safety in emergency, and the worse the smash if an accident happens. Always be able to pull up well within the distance you can see is clear. (See inside back cover).

50 Never accelerate when being overtaken.

SPEED LIMIT

51 A speed limit is imposed for reasons of safety which may not always be obvious. To exceed it is to take a risk, as well as being an offence. (See pages 20 and 24).

NIGHT DRIVING

At night always drive well within the limits of your **52**
lights. If you are dazzled, slow down even to a
standstill.

VEHICLE CONDITION

Make sure that your vehicle is in a fit condition to **53**
be used on the road. Give regular attention to
brakes, steering and tyres. Do not wait for an
accident.

 If you drive a MOTOR VEHICLE *study
this Section and Paragraphs* 22-53.

DOORS

Before opening any door of a vehicle, make sure **54**
that the vehicle has stopped and that you will not
endanger or inconvenience anyone on the road or
footpath.

DIRECTION INDICATORS

If you use a direction indicator, see that it is returned **55**
to neutral as soon as your movement is completed.

MIRRORS

Make a habit of using your driving mirror so that **56**
you know what is behind you, especially when
about to move off, turn, overtake, stop, or open the
door.

IN CONVOY

If you are a driver in a convoy, or a driver of one of **57**
a series of large vehicles such as lorries or motor
coaches, do not drive close behind the vehicle in
front of you. Leave ample space so that a faster

vehicle after overtaking you can, if necessary, draw in to the left again before overtaking the next vehicle.

HEADLIGHTS

58 Do not use your headlights unnecessarily, especially in lighted areas.

59 Dip your headlights when meeting other vehicles on the road unless there are exceptional circumstances which make it unsafe for you to do so.

60 Switch off or dip your headlights when you are following close behind another vehicle which you do not intend to overtake.

61 When your headlights are dipped or extinguished be specially careful.

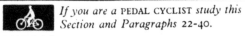 *If you are a* PEDAL CYCLIST *study this Section and Paragraphs* 22-40.

GENERAL

62 Ride in single file when road or traffic conditions require it, and never more than two abreast.

63 Do not wobble about the road. (See page 30).

64 When traffic is held up do not take risks by riding along a narrow space between vehicles.

65 Never ride close behind a fast moving vehicle; it may slow down or stop suddenly.

66 Do not hold on to another vehicle. (See page 27).

67 Make sure that your rear light, reflector and white patch are kept clean and are never obscured by your clothing or anything else.

CONTROL OF MACHINE

68 Keep full control of your cycle.

69 Do not ride a machine which is too big for you.

Do not carry a passenger on your cycle unless it is **70** constructed or adapted for the purpose. (See page 27).

Never carry parcels or other articles which may **71** interfere with the proper control of your machine, or may cause harm to others.

Take special care in bad weather and on slippery **72** roads. If you fall you may be run over.

Cross tramlines at a wide angle and signal your **73** intention well in advance.

CYCLE TRACKS
If there is a cycle track — use it. **74**

VEHICLE CONDITION
Make sure that your cycle is in a fit condition to be **75** used on the road, and in particular that the brakes act properly. (See page 31).

 If you ride a HORSE *or are in* CHARGE OF HORSES OR OTHER ANIMALS *study this Section.*

When leading an animal, always place yourself **76** between it and the traffic and keep the animal to the edge of the road. This rule applies equally whether you are walking or riding. When leading an animal do not ride a bicycle.

If you are a drover, and have another person with **77** you, send him on ahead so that he can warn traffic, particularly at a bend or a brow of a hill, or when animals are coming out of a gateway on to a road.

Make sure the road is clear before you let an **78** animal out of a field or yard on to the road.

13

Signals to be given by Police
Constables and others

engaged in the regulation of traffic, as viewed by the driver for whom they are intended.

"Stop" signal (vehicle approaching from the front).

"Stop" signal (vehicle approaching from behind).

"Stop" signal (vehicles approaching from the front and from behind simultaneously).

Drivers should note that, after they have stopped, the Police Constable may lower his hand or use it for giving other signals, but they must not move on until signalled to do so.

Release Signals, given according to circumstances, are shown below.

To bring on a vehicle from the front. (A beckoning movement.)

To bring on a vehicle from behind.

To bring on vehicles from right or left. (A beckoning movement.)

Drivers should be specially careful to distinguish the "Proceed" signal, intended for them, from signals intended for other traffic. This will be shown primarily by the Constable looking in their direction.

Signals to be given by drivers and cyclists *to indicate their own intentions, where a mechanical indicator is not used.*

These signals are for the purpose of giving information *and not instructions* to others. The arm should be extended beyond the side of the vehicle at least as far as the elbow.

SIGNALS TO OTHER DRIVERS

" I am going to SLOW DOWN or STOP."

" I am going to TURN to my RIGHT."

" I am READY to be OVERTAKEN."

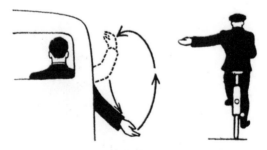

" I am going to TURN to my LEFT."

Alternative signals which may be used by drivers of horse-drawn vehicles.

" I am going to STOP."

" I am going to TURN."

After rotating the whip, incline it to the right or left to show the direction in which the turn is to be made.

Signals by drivers to Police Constables.

When approaching a Police Constable engaged in regulating traffic, drivers should, whenever possible, indicate to him the direction in which they wish to proceed. Signals for this purpose are shown below.

" I want to go **STRAIGHT AHEAD.**"

"I want to **TURN** to my **LEFT.**"

"I want to **TURN** to my **RIGHT.**"

Traffic Signs and Signals

The following are some of the more important of the traffic signs, and all road users should be familiar with their significance.

Red

Where the speed limit begins this sign is used.

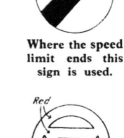

Where the speed limit ends this sign is used.

Red

HALT
AT
MAJOR
ROAD
AHEAD

Red

SLOW

MAJOR
ROAD
AHEAD

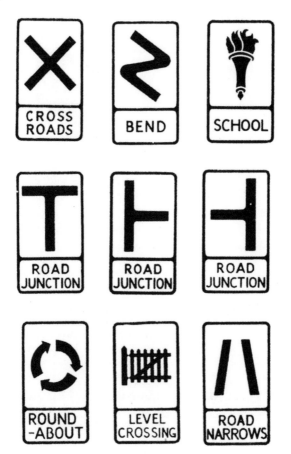

CROSS ROADS

BEND

SCHOOL

ROAD JUNCTION

ROAD JUNCTION

ROAD JUNCTION

ROUND-ABOUT

LEVEL CROSSING

ROAD NARROWS

HILL
1 IN 12

HUMP
BRIDGE

TRAFFIC LIGHT SIGNALS

RED . . . . means STOP and wait behind the stop line on the carriageway.

RED AND AMBER means STOP but be prepared to go when the Green shows.

GREEN . . . . means PROCEED if the road is clear but with particular care if the intention is to turn right or left.

AMBER . . . . means STOP at the stop line unless the Amber signal appears when you have already passed the stop line or are so close to it that to pull up might cause an accident.

GREEN ARROW shown with the RED signal allows vehicles to proceed in the direction indicated by the arrow.

The Law's Demands

This is not a complete list, but it sets out some of the main demands of the law upon road users. For complete information you should refer to the various Acts and Regulations. In these notes the following abbreviations are used :

C. & U.R.	..	Motor Vehicles (Construction and Use) Regulations.
D.L.R.	..	Motor Vehicles (Driving Licences) Regulations.
H.A. ..	..	Highway Act.
P.C.P.R.	..	Pedestrian Crossing Places (Traffic) Regulations.
R.T.A.	..	Road Traffic Act.
R.T.L.A.	..	Road Transport Lighting Act.
R.V.L.R.	..	Road Vehicles Lighting Regulations.

TO DRIVERS OF ALL MOTOR VEHICLES

BEFORE DRIVING make sure that—

Your vehicle is properly licensed (Roads Act, 1920, sections 8 and 9, and Finance Act, 1920, section 13, as amended).

Your insurance is in order.

You must be insured against claims for personal injuries to third parties. If you allow another person to drive your vehicle you must satisfy yourself that your insurance policy, or his, covers the particular use of the vehicle while he is driving it (R.T.A., 1930, section 35). A certificate of insurance must be obtained from an authorised insurer and must be produced to a police constable on demand. If it is not so produced, it must be produced in person within five days at a police station specified at the time the certificate is demanded (R.T.A., 1930, sections 36 (5) and 40 (1)).

23

Your driving licence is not out of date and that you have signed it (R.T.A., 1930, section 4 (1), and D.L.R., 1937, No. 17).

You are in a fit condition to drive and are not under the influence of drink or drug (R.T.A., 1930, section 15).

Your vehicle is in a roadworthy condition :—

Brakes
Steering gear $\left\{\begin{array}{l}\text{must be in good working order and}\\ \text{properly adjusted (C. & U.R., 1941,}\\ \text{No. 68).}\end{array}\right.$

Tyres must be free from defect likely to cause danger to anyone or damage to the road (C. & U.R., 1941, No. 71).

Windscreen must be kept clean and the windscreen wiper in working order (C. & U.R., 1941, Nos. 72 and 68).

Mirror must be properly adjusted (C. & U.R., 1941, No. 15).

Warning instrument must be in working order (C. & U.R., 1941, No. 18).

It must not be sounded in built-up areas at night (11.30 p.m. to 7 a.m.), nor on any road when the vehicle is stationary (C. & U.R., 1941, Nos. 78 and 79).

Silencer, etc.—There must be no excessive noise due to an inefficient silencer or to defects or lack of repair (C. & U.R., 1941, Nos. 69 and 75).

All parts and accessories must be in such condition that no danger is likely to be caused to anyone (C. & U.R., 1941, No. 67 (1)).

Your lights are functioning (R.T.L.A., 1927, section 1)

Your load is $\left\{\begin{array}{l}\text{of such weight}\\ \text{so distributed}\\ \text{so adjusted}\\ \text{so secured}\end{array}\right\}$ that danger will not arise.

(C. & U.R., 1941, No. 67 (1) and (2)).

WHEN DRIVING

You must

observe speed limits (R.T.A., 1930, section 10 and 1st Sch. R.T.A., 1934, section 1, etc.) ;

observe traffic signals and signs (R.T.A., 1930, section 49) ;
observe police officers' directions (R.T.A., 1930, section 49)
and respect pedestrian crossings (P.C.P.R., 1941, Nos. 3-5,
see also " Pedestrian Crossings " page 28);

see that your obligatory lamps are alight at night (R.T.L.A.,
1927, section 1).

You must not
drive recklessly (R.T.A., 1930, section 11) ;

drive in a manner or at a speed dangerous to the public
(R.T.A., 1930, section 11) ;

drive without due care and attention (R.T.A., 1930,
section 12) ;

drive without reasonable consideration for other persons
using the road (R.T.A., 1930, section 12) ;

drive under the influence of drink or a drug (R.T.A., 1930,
section 15);

be in a position which prevents you from having proper
control of the vehicle, or a full view ahead (C. & U.R., 1941,
No. 82 (2)).

WHEN YOU STOP
You must
stop the engine and set the brake, if you leave the vehicle
(C. & U.R., 1941, No. 82 (3)) ;

at night, turn off your headlights (unless you have to
stop owing to traffic conditions) but see that the obligatory
lamps are alight (R.V.L.R., 1936, No. 12, and R.T.L.A.,
1927, section 1) ;

You must not
leave your vehicle in a position where danger or obstruction
is likely to arise or on a pedestrian crossing (R.T.A., 1930,
section 50; H.A., 1835, section 72; C. & U.R., 1941, No. 81;
P.C.P.R., 1941, No. 6) ;

sound your horn while stationary (C. & U.R., 1941, No. 79).

IF YOU ARE INVOLVED IN AN ACCIDENT
You must
   (i) stop ; and

(ii) give your own and the vehicle owner's name and address and the index mark of the vehicle to a police constable or anyone having reasonable grounds for wanting these particulars ; and

(iii) if a person is injured, produce your certificate of insurance or security to a police constable or anyone who has with reasonable grounds required its production.

You must

report the accident to a police constable or at a police station as soon as practicable and in any case within 24 hours in the following circumstances : if, for any reason, you have not supplied your identifying particulars as in (ii) above, and, in injury cases, if you have not produced your certificate as in (iii) above (R.T.A., 1930, sections 22 and 40 (2)).

TO MOTOR CYCLISTS

Most of the foregoing requirements apply to you. In addition—

You must not

carry more than one passenger on a two-wheeled machine, and the passenger must sit astride the cycle on a proper seat securely fixed behind the driver's seat (R.T.A., 1930, section 16).

TO DRIVERS OF HORSE-DRAWN VEHICLES

You must

hold the reins, unless your horse is conducted by someone else (H.A., 1835, section 78) ;

observe traffic signals and signs (R.T.A., 1930, section 49) ;

observe police officers' directions (R.T.A., 1930, section 49) ;

respect pedestrian crossings (P.C.P.R., 1941, Nos. 3-5 see also " Pedestrian Crossings " page 28) ;

at night, see that your lamps are alight (R.T.L.A., 1927, section 1).

You must not

drive furiously so as to endanger the life or limb of anyone, including yourself (H.A., 1835, section 78) ;

be so far away from your horse that you have not control over it (H.A., 1835, section 78) ;

drive if you are drunk (Licensing Act, 1872, section 12) ;

leave your vehicle in a position where danger or obstruction is likely to arise, or on a pedestrian crossing (R.T.A., 1930, section 50 ; H.A., 1835, section 72 ; P.C.P.R., 1941, No. 6).

TO PEDAL CYCLISTS

You must

observe traffic signals and signs (R.T.A., 1930, section 49) ;

observe police officers' directions (R.T.A., 1930, section 49) ;

respect pedestrian crossings (P.C.P.R., 1941, Nos. 3-5, see also " Pedestrian Crossings " page 28) ;

at night, see that your lamps are alight (R.T.L.A., 1927, sections 1 and 5).

You must not

ride furiously so as to endanger the life or limb of anyone, including yourself (H.A., 1835, section 78) ;

ride if you are drunk (Licensing Act, 1872, section 12) ;

ride on a footway or footpath by the side of any road made or set apart for the use of foot passengers (H.A., 1835, section 72) ;

carry a passenger if your cycle is not constructed or adapted to carry more than one person (R.T.A., 1934, section 20) ;

hold on to a motor vehicle or trailer in motion, without lawful authority or reasonable cause (R.T.A., 1930, section 29).

TO PEDESTRIANS

You must not

wilfully cause obstruction of the footway or highway (H.A., 1835, section 72);

loiter on a pedestrian crossing (P.C.P.R., 1941, No. 7, see also " Pedestrian Crossings " below);

without lawful authority or reasonable excuse—hold or get on to a motor vehicle or trailer in motion; tamper with the brake or other part of the mechanism of a stationary vehicle (R.T.A., 1930, section 29).

be drunk in any highway or public place (Licensing Act, 1872, section 12).

PEDESTRIAN CROSSINGS

It is an offence under the Pedestrian Crossing Places (Traffic) Regulations to disobey the following requirements—

(1) **Drivers of vehicles, and cyclists**

    (a) When you are approaching a pedestrian crossing, proceed at a speed which will enable you to stop before reaching the crossing, unless you can see that there is no pedestrian on the crossing.

    (b) Where a pedestrian crossing is controlled by police or light signals, allow free passage to any pedestrian who has started to cross before you receive the signal to proceed.

    (c) Where a pedestrian crossing is not controlled by police or by light signals, give way to any pedestrian on the crossing.

    (d) Never stop on any pedestrian crossing unless you are forced to do so by circumstances beyond your control or to avoid an accident.

(2) **Pedestrians**

A pedestrian may not remain on a pedestrian crossing longer than is necessary for the purpose of passing from one side of the road to the other with reasonable despatch.

Hints on Driving

SOME GENERAL HINTS

See that your driving seat is secure and correctly adjusted before moving off.

Make sure your tyres are in good condition and inflated to the correct pressure. A front or rear burst is dangerous, but the former is the more disastrous.

When driving, keep both hands on the steering wheel unless you are performing a necessary driving function.

Never drive with your elbow on the window ledge—it restricts your movements in an emergency.

Keep a sharp look-out for changes in road condition. Learn to notice quickly and use extra care where the camber of a road is against you or where the surface is loose, greasy, icy, highly polished, or covered with leaves.

Unless compelled by traffic conditions, avoid driving closely behind the vehicle in front of you. If you do, your vision is restricted and your margin of safety lessened; should the driver in front suddenly brake or swerve.

When following a 'bus or tramcar, look ahead for the stopping places, as these will warn you of the likelihood of such a vehicle pulling up or the possibility of persons suddenly crossing the road to board it.

Keep a look out on both sides of the road as well as to your front.

Learn to look well ahead so that you will see road signs and warnings of danger in sufficient time for you to be able to react.

Never brake or accelerate violently at a corner: it may induce skidding.

29

Don't start making adjustments while travelling—stop and make them in safety.

Be very careful at night when approaching red " danger " lamps on the road. There may have been an accident and people may walk unexpectedly 1. to the path of your vehicle.

At night a " flick " on or off of your headlights is a useful form of warning at cross roads or to traffic which you are overtaking.

A good driver, though he may use different controls in quick succession, should be very observant and never allow himself to be placed in such a position that he must try to do too many things at the same time. His whole method of driving should be mapped out. It should be deliberate and thoughtful, which means that he should never need to be hurried, as he must always be master of his machine. In other words, he should be competent to drive it, and be equally competent in controlling himself. Always concentrate on your driving.

Hints on Cycling

The Highway Code tells you the principles of good roadmanship. But it does not always tell you what those principles involve, because it does not deal with the " technicalities " of cycling.

You are told not to wobble about the road. A common cause of wobbling is riding a machine that is too big for the rider. It is advisable, when practicable, for the saddle to be so adjusted that, to avoid dismounting, the rider can place one foot to the ground when the cycle is stationary.

Another possible cause of wobbling is pedalling with the " waist " of the foot on the pedal : at slow speeds, or when turning a corner, the toe may catch the front mudguard and cause an unintentional and uncontrolled swerve.

Keeping full control of the cycle implies three things. First, that the machine is in mechanically good condition ; second, that it is the right size ; and third, that the rider has road sense.

A CYCLE IS NOT IN GOOD CONDITION

If
- *the bearings are too slack ;*
- *the brakes are not fully effective ;*
- *the wheels are out of line ;*
- *spokes are loose or missing ;*
- *the chain is slack ;*
- *the mudguards are not firmly attached ;*
- *the handlebar or saddle is not secure ;*
- *the tyres are badly worn or soft.*

Before descending a steep hill make sure, by a touch of the brakes, that they are working properly.

Have your bell in such a position that you are able to ring it and at the same time apply your brakes.

Even when facing a strong wind or driving rain, keep your eyes on the road ahead.

Take special care in bad weather or on slippery roads. In foggy weather be prepared to deal with emergencies that would not arise in normal conditions, *e.g.*, finding a vehicle on the wrong side of the road or a pedestrian " lost " on the highway.

In very windy weather be prepared for sudden gusts which may cause you to swerve (especially if you are wearing a cape), particularly at road junctions.

Never apply your front brake first, especially when the road surface is wet or rough, as this tends to cause a front-wheel skid, which is almost impossible to correct ; sudden changes of direction on wet roads should be avoided, because of the risk of side-slip.

This Code is issued with the Authority of Parliament
(Resolutions passed July 1946)

'' A failure on the part of any person to observe any provision of the highway code shall not of itself render that person liable to criminal proceedings of any kind, but any such failure may in any proceedings (whether civil or criminal, and including proceedings for an offence under this Act) be relied upon by any party to the proceedings as tending to establish or to negative any liability which is in question in those proceedings.''

[*Road Traffic Act*, 1930, *Section* 45]

70598   Wt. 2784   51-2243   4,500M   9/46   H. & S. Ltd.

STUDY THE FOLLOWING TABLE AND THINK IN TERMS OF OVERALL STOPPING DISTANCE

This is what proper BRAKES can do on good Dry Level Surfaces.

SPEED M.P.H.	THINKING DISTANCE	BRAKING DISTANCE	OVERALL STOPPING DISTANCE
	Feet	Feet	Feet
10	10	5	15
20	20	20	40
30	30	45	75
40	40	80	120
50	50	125	175

THINKING DISTANCE = Distance travelled before driver reacts.

BRAKING DISTANCE = Distance travelled after driver applies brakes.

DO YOU REALISE how long it takes to pull up a car in an emergency? This table is based on the assumption that the driver reacts quickly, and that the brakes and road surface are in good condition. The overall stopping distances indicated represent the least margin of safety which can be allowed at different speeds from 10 to 50 miles per hour. Remember that the distances are greatly increased if road or weather conditions are bad or if your vehicle is not in first-class condition. On a skiddy road the braking distances should at least be doubled.

THE

HIGHWAY

CODE

To be purchased direct from
H.M. STATIONERY OFFICE
at the following addresses:

WITH AN APPENDIX
INCLUDING DIAGRAMS
OF SIGNALS AND SIGNS

YORK HOUSE, KINGSWAY, LONDON, W.C.2: 13ᴬ CAS
STREET, EDINBURGH 2: 39-41 KING STREET, MANCHESTE
1 ST. ANDREW'S CRESCENT. CARDIFF: 80 CHICHES
STREET. BELFAST. OR THROUGH ANY BOOKSELL

55.

THE 1954 HIGHWAY CODE

By 1954, the hardships suffered in Britain as a result of the Second World War were starting to fade in the face of a growing optimism for the future. The last of the post-war ration coupons were consigned to the dustbin as meat became the final item to be derationed.

This was a brave new world with jet airliners, new homes were being built in Britain at a rate of around 30,000 a year and the nation's flag flew on the roof of the world, Sir Edmund Hillary having conquered Mount Everest in 1953 just a few days before the young Queen Elizabeth II took the throne.

The Goon Show was attracting record audiences on the radio and more than 3.25 million homes in Britain had television sets in time to watch 1954's live broadcasts of *The World Cup* from Switzerland. The government passed a bill paving the way for commercial television, you could buy a new Ford Popular for £390 (including purchase tax) and smog masks were available on the NHS.

Into this thoroughly modern Britain in 1954 was published the fourth edition of *The Highway Code*, also demonstrating an end to the austerity years by returning to its pre-war size.

Front cover of the 1954 *Highway Code*.

The Code in Colour

The facsimile reproduction that begins on page 93 of this book is, slightly confusingly, the third edition of the fourth edition which was issued in 1957 and includes some minor revisions to keep *The Highway Code* up to date with changes in the law.

The most noticeable overall difference, however, between the 1954 *Highway Code* and its predecessors is that this was the first year that the booklet was printed using colour. Once the consumer had taken in that major change, the next thing to notice was that the price had gone up to sixpence ($2^{1}/_{2}$p), when it had previously been only a penny.

While the background colour on the new front cover was a rather dull grey, it served to highlight the red and green discs that were part of its design. The discs were stylized traffic lights which were, by then, a common sight at road junctions in towns and cities all over the country. Inside, the new booklet boasted the first ever *Highway Code* colour diagrams explaining the traffic-light sequence.

The Zebra Crossing

The booklet also contained an illustration showing the new Zebra Crossing. Since the mid-1930s, certain pedestrian crossings had been marked by orange globes mounted on poles at the edge of the pavement. These were known as Belisha Beacons, having been named after the then Minister of Transport, Leslie Hore-Belisha.

It was found that pedestrians needed greater encouragement to seek out the new crossing points and, in the late 1940s, a handful of experimental high-visibility crossings were tested. These had black and white stripes painted on the road, although red and white markings had been considered, with an illuminated orange globe atop a black-and-white-striped pole at each kerbside.

In April 1949 1,000 such crossings were marked on roads around the country as part of Pedestrian Crossing Week and in 1951 the Zebra Crossing was officially ratified, with 'no stopping' zones on either side of the crossing and pedestrians having precedence on the crossing itself.

Three ladies prepare to try out a recently-installed Zebra Crossing in the early fifties.

Tufty Fluffytail

Road safety initiatives such as this were sorely needed. There were 57,000 pedestrians injured in 1951 and of the 5,010 people who died on Britain's roads that year, 2,400 were on foot. Almost eighty per cent of the pedestrians killed were either elderly people or children. The Royal Society for the Prevention of Accidents, by now more commonly known as ROSPA, had introduced the 'Kerb Drill' for children in 1942, which included the mantra 'Look right, look left, look right again'.

ROSPA also promoted National Child Safety Week in 1950, a campaign that saw child road fatalities fall to their lowest level for twenty-five years. In 1952 they launched The Teddy Club to teach road safety to children under the age of six, and the following year Tufty Fluffytail made his first appearance in a series of ROSPA children's stories designed to make youngsters aware of the dangers involved in crossing the road. By 1961 Tufty would have his own Tufty Club and today he even has his own website.

The endearing appeal of such cuddly characters was offset by ROSPA's first 'shock' poster campaign which featured an image of a young boy on crutches, one of his legs having been amputated. Another of the posters stressed the danger of drinking and driving, and a special warning about alcohol was included on the inside cover of the new *Code*.

Doctors had recognized drinking and driving as a major cause of accidents and in 1954 called for more stringent roadside tests for those suspected of being drunk, with walking a white line or reciting a tongue twister being dismissed as inadequate. The first breathalyser was invented in America in 1954 but would not be used in Britain until 1967.

As Britain's road system became more crowded, the number of fatalities grew, peaking at almost 8,000 in 1966, although a significant downward trend would not be seen until 1974.

In 1952, this Salford police car helped to promote a local road safety initiative.

First Aid Instructions

One of several innovations in 1954's thirty-two-page booklet was a set of first aid instructions laid out in strident red and green type over a bright yellow background on the back cover.

Listed as 'Guidance For The Untrained', they detailed a few basic steps that should be taken in the event of an accident, forming a very handy checklist for any motorists who carried their copy of the *Code* in their glove compartment. The expanded version of this advice in the modern *Highway Code* is inconveniently hidden away inside on page 131.

Safer Vehicles on the Road

The 1954 *Highway Code* devoted more space than ever before to pointing out 'The Law's Demands'. Since the 1937 Motor Vehicles Construction and Use Regulations had been introduced, vehicle windscreens had to be made from safety glass (although still a far cry from modern laminated glass), automatic wipers were required and brakes and steering had to be maintained in good condition.

Further rules soon followed, yet vehicles did not have to undergo regular official tests to ensure that they were road legal until the Ministry of Transport 'MoT' test was eventually introduced in 1960.

In the meantime, vehicle safety features continued to be introduced almost on an ad hoc basis. Flashing indicator lights, for example, became legal in 1954 but were not legally required on new cars in Britain until nine years later. *The Highway Code* was there to help everyone keep track of the changes, and more people than ever before had need of it.

When the driving test was introduced in 1935, of the 246,000 who took the test, fewer than 155,000 passed. Twenty years later, almost 920,000 learner drivers sat their tests, with around 434,000 gaining their full driving licence.

Motorway Madness

Twice as many road signs appeared in the 1954 *Highway Code* than previously, but there were still only a fraction of the number that appear in today's version. We now have an entire regiment of road signs that were simply not required in the mid-fifties – motorway signs. Britain's first motorway, the Preston Bypass section of what would become the M6, was not opened until 1958. The first section of the M1 followed almost a year later.

There were no speed limits on the new motorways, which were said to have been designed to cope with vehicles travelling at up to 100 mph, but, following a series of horrendous pile-ups in thick fog, the 70 mph speed limit was set in 1965. The first *Highway Code* booklet to make any mention of motorways or motorway signage would be the fifth edition in 1959.

Children playing in the street were a driver's worst nightmare.

The Friendly Policeman

The design of the 1954 booklet was as different from the 1946 edition as that version had been from the ones that had preceded it, but the idea of using icons to separate and identify information relevant to pedestrians, cyclists, motorcyclists and drivers was retained. The icons themselves were updated in a more modern style as black silhouettes rather than white-on-black images, but they served the same purpose.

Similarly, the motorist demonstrating hand signals was redesigned, benefiting from a more modern-looking car and, where his face was visible, a friendly smile. The new contemporary graphic style was also applied to the policeman, who was now looking very pleased with himself.

Just as these old *Highway Code* booklets look rather quaint to us in the twenty-first century, today's version would look almost completely alien to a road user magically transported forward in time from 1931.

The purpose of *The Highway Code*, however, is unchanged. In the introduction to the latest edition, it states that 'Knowing and applying the rules contained in The Highway Code could significantly reduce road casualties. Cutting the number of deaths and injuries that occur on our roads every day is a responsibility we all share.'

The message hammered home by *The Highway Code* after more than seventy years remains the same.

GO

COME ON
Beckoning on a vehicle from front

COME ON
Beckoning on a vehicle from behind

COME ON
Beckoning on a vehicle from the side

By 1954, the policeman directing traffic had something to smile about.

THE

HIGHWAY

CODE

HER MAJESTY'S STATIONERY OFFICE   PRICE 6D NET

Remember

CHILDREN are in special danger—particularly those under five and those who cycle. Protect them and train them in road safety.

OLD PEOPLE may react slowly. Give them great consideration.

HEALTH counts. Make due allowance for poor eyesight, deafness and fatigue.

ALCOHOL even in quite small amounts, makes you less safe on the roads. Be sure you are fit to use them.

VEHICLES badly maintained may lead to an accident. Check your lights, brakes, steering and tyres.

Issued by the Ministry of Transport and Civil Aviation

The Highway Code, as it now appears, has been framed to take into account the many helpful comments which were made on the earlier versions by Members of Parliament, the Press, and by many motorists, cyclists, and pedestrians. As it now stands I think it does embody the practical experience of many road-users of all kinds. This is as it should be, for its purpose is that it should be of help to all who use our roads.

The Highway Code is not a body of law, with pains and penalties to back it. It is a collection of Do's and Don'ts for drivers, cyclists and pedestrians based on good manners and good sense. These matter perhaps more on the roads than anywhere else. If we ignore them we can so easily come to grief ourselves or, still worse, kill or maim somebody else. We can in a split second do something which we will regret all our lives.

The Highway Code is designed to help to make our roads safer. If we follow it in the spirit and in the letter we can each of us contribute very directly to keeping down the number of accidents and to keeping traffic on our roads flowing smoothly.

A lot of hard work and hard thought has gone into producing this Highway Code. It can give a lot of help to those who study it and really try to follow it. I am sure all sensible and public-spirited people will.

Minister of Transport
and Civil Aviation

1954

I

CONTENTS

THE HIGHWAY CODE

Appendix: Signs and Signals

THE LAW'S DEMANDS

THE

HIGHWAY CODE

This Code, between pages 4 and 26, is issued with the
Authority of Parliament
(Resolutions passed November 1954)

★

" A failure on the part of any person to observe
any provision of the highway code shall not of
itself render that person liable to criminal
proceedings of any kind, but any such failure
may in any proceedings (whether civil or
criminal, and including proceedings for an
offence under this Act) be relied upon by any
party to the proceedings as tending to establish
or to negative any liability which is in question
in those proceedings."

ROAD TRAFFIC ACT, 1930.   SECTION 45.

PART 1

THE ROAD USER ON FOOT

1. Where there is a pavement or footpath, use it.

Walking Along

2. On a pavement or footpath, do not walk next to the kerb with your back to the traffic.

3. Where there is no footpath, walk on the right of the road to face oncoming traffic.

4. A marching body which cannot use a footpath should keep on the left-hand side of the road. It should have a look-out at suitable distances at the front and rear, and at night the look-outs should carry lights, white at the front of the column and red at the rear.

5. Do not walk along cycle tracks.

*　　　　*　　　　*

Crossing the Road

6. Before you cross the road, *stop at the kerb, look right, look left, and right again.* Do not cross until the road is clear ; then cross at right-angles, keeping a careful look-out all the time. If there is a refuge, stop on it and look again. On one-way traffic roads, stop and look towards oncoming traffic before you cross.

7. Do not cross unless you have a clear view of the road both ways. Take extra care near stationary vehicles or other obstructions, and whenever your view is limited.

8. Do not climb over or through guard rails.

Crossing the road carelessly contributes to
23,000 accidents a year. (*"Accidents", in these footnotes, are those in which someone was killed or injured.*)

9. Where there is a pedestrian crossing, refuge, footbridge or subway, use it.

10. Observe these rules about PEDESTRIAN CROSSINGS:

(*a*) When you have stepped off the kerb on to a zebra crossing (which must have black and white stripes, studs and lighted beacons), you have the right of way UNLESS A POLICE OFFICER IS CONTROLLING TRAFFIC OVER IT. But be sensible ; wait for a suitable gap in the traffic so that drivers have time to give way.

(*b*) If a police officer is in charge, watch for his signals and do not cross until he holds up the traffic.

(*c*) At a crossing controlled by traffic lights— with studs but no stripes—do not cross in front of traffic which has the signal to proceed.

11. Where traffic lights have a " Cross Now " signal, wait until that signal appears before you cross.

12. If there is a police officer controlling traffic, be guided by his signals.

13. At every road junction, look out for traffic turning the corner.

14. Never loiter in the roadway.

*   *   *

Getting on or off Public Vehicles   **15.** Do not get on or off a bus or tram while it is moving, or when it is not at a recognised stopping place. If you want to get on a bus or tram at a request stop, give a clear signal for it to stop and do not step into the road until it has stopped.

Getting on or off public vehicles without due care contributes to 7,500 accidents a year.

PART 2

THE ROAD USER ON WHEELS

TO ALL DRIVERS AND RIDERS and in general to those in charge of horses.

Driving Along

16. Before you move off, make sure that you can do so safely and without inconvenience to other road users. Watch particularly the road behind. Make the proper signal before moving out, and give way to passing and overtaking vehicles.

17. KEEP WELL TO THE LEFT, except when you intend to overtake or turn right. Do not hug the middle of the road.

18. Never drive at such a speed that you cannot pull up well within the distance you can see to be clear. Always leave yourself enough room in which to stop. At night, always drive well within the limit of your lights.

19. If you are dazzled, slow down or stop.

20. Go slowly on roads under repair.

21. Slow down before a blind or sharp bend.

*　　　　*　　　　*

The Safety of Pedestrians

22. Give way to pedestrians on uncontrolled zebra crossings. *They have the right of way.* Signal to other drivers your intention to slow down or stop.

23. At pedestrian crossings controlled by light signals or by the police, give way to pedestrians already on the crossings when the signal to move is given.

Going too fast contributes to 7,500 accidents a year.

24. Watch for the pedestrian who comes out suddenly from beyond stationary vehicles and other obstructions. Be specially careful of this near schools, bus and tram stopping places and pedestrian crossings.

25. Give way to pedestrians about to get on or off a tramcar.

26. Go slowly when passing animals and give them plenty of room. Stop if necessary or if signalled to do so. Be prepared to meet pedestrians and led animals coming towards you on your side of the road, especially on a left-hand bend.

*　　　　*　　　　*

Signals **27.** Give signals of your intentions correctly, clearly and IN GOOD TIME.

*　　　　*　　　　*

Overtaking **28.** Never overtake unless you KNOW that you can do so without danger to yourself or others. Be specially careful at dusk, and in fog or mist, when it is more difficult to judge speed and distance.

29. Do not overtake at or near
- **—a corner or bend**
- **—a road junction**
- **—a pedestrian crossing**

Do not overtake when approaching
- **—the brow of a hill**
- **—a hump-back bridge**

Do not overtake
- **—where the road narrows**
- **—or when to do so would force other vehicles to swerve or to reduce speed.**

IF IN DOUBT—HOLD BACK.

Overtaking improperly and misjudging clearance, distance or speed, contribute to 20,000 accidents a year.

30. Overtake on the right except when the driver in front has signalled that he intends to turn right. (This does not necessarily apply at roundabouts, or on one-way roads, or when overtaking tramcars.)

31. Never pull out sharply from the nearside but always give ample warning. Never cut in, that is, do not pull in sharply in front of a moving vehicle which you have just overtaken.

32. Never cross a continuous white line along the middle of the road unless you can see the road well ahead and know that it is clear.

33. In traffic hold-ups, keep in your own lane.

*　　　　*　　　　*

Road Junctions　**34.** When approaching a road junction where there is a " SLOW " sign, slow down and be ready to stop when you get there.

35. Where there is a " HALT " sign, you must stop at the major road ahead even if there is no traffic on it.

36. At a road junction, look right, then left, then right again. Do not go on until you are sure that it is safe to do so.

37. At a road junction, give way to traffic on the major road. If in doubt, give way.

38. Do not rely on signals to go ahead given by unauthorised persons.

*　　　　*　　　　*

Railway Level Crossings　**39.** At ungated railway level crossings with signs, slow down, look both ways, listen and make sure it is safe before crossing the lines.

Drivers crossing road junctions carelessly contribute to 11,000 accidents a year.

40. At gated but unmanned railway level crossings, first open *both* gates. Look both ways, listen, and make sure it is safe before crossing the lines. Never stop your vehicle on the crossing. Close the gates after you have crossed.

*   *   *

Turning Corners

41. If you intend to turn right, signal in good time and take up a position just left of the middle of the road.

42. If you intend to turn left, keep over to the left, give the turn-left signal in good time, and do not swing out to the right.

43. When turning from one road into another make the turn carefully and show consideration to pedestrians.

44. When held up at a road junction by police or light signal, do not " filter " left unless you receive a definite signal to do so.

45. Let the police officer controlling traffic know clearly by your signal which way you want to go.

*   *   *

Stopping

46. When you draw up, pull in close to the near-side of the road. If you are ready to be overtaken, give the appropriate signal.

EXTRA RULES FOR PEDAL CYCLISTS

47. Glance behind before you signal, move off, change course, overtake or turn.

48. If there is an adequate cycle track, use it.

49. Never ride more than two abreast on the carriageway.

Turning right without due care contributes to 12,000 accidents a year.

50. Never carry anything that may interfere with the proper control of your machine.

51. Do not hold on to another vehicle or another cyclist.

52. Do not ride close behind a moving vehicle.

EXTRA RULES FOR DRIVERS OF MOTOR VEHICLES AND RIDERS OF MOTOR CYCLES AND MOTOR-ASSISTED PEDAL CYCLES

Traffic Behind You **53.** If you are a driver, and you want to move off, or reverse, or open your door, look round and make sure that no one is about to overtake you and that there are no children or obstructions in the " blind area " near your front or back wheels.

54. If a driver, look in your driving mirror before you signal or change course, or overtake, or turn, or stop.

55. If riding a motor cycle, *even one fitted with a mirror*, glance behind before you signal, or move off, or change course, or overtake, or turn.

*   *   *

Driving Along **56.** Do not drive nose to tail when on the open road.

57. Do not accelerate when being overtaken.

58. If a vehicle you are overtaking does accelerate, do not race it but fall behind.

Inattention or diverted attention contributes to 11,000 accidents a year.

Night Driving

59. After dark, do not rely on sidelights in built-up areas unless the street lighting is good : on unlighted roads, do not drive on sidelights only.

60. When meeting other vehicles and cyclists, dip your headlights whenever road and traffic conditions allow you to do so.

61. When following closely behind another vehicle, dip your headlights.

*   *   *

Direction Indicators

62. Make sure that your direction indicator has given the signal intended, and that it is cancelled immediately after use.

*   *   *

Reversing

63. Do not reverse from a side road into a main road. To turn round in a main road, reverse into a convenient side road, preferably one on your left, and make sure that the main road is clear before you re-enter it.

64. If you are driving a large vehicle and your view to the rear is restricted, get help when reversing.

*   *   *

Parking and Stopping

65. Do not let your vehicle stand in the carriageway :

(*a*) in a main road if you can park in a car park, lay-by or in a suitable side street ;

(*b*) on any road carrying fast-moving traffic ;

(*c*) opposite, or nearly opposite, a standing vehicle ;

(*d*) alongside a standing vehicle, thus causing " double-banking " ;

(*e*) opposite a refuge, road repairs, or other obstruction ;

Negligence when reversing and turning round in the road contributes to 3,000 accidents a year.

(*f*) where there is a continuous white line ;

(*g*) near a bus or tram stop or school entrance ;

(*h*) near a road junction or a bend ;

(*i*) near the brow of a hill or a hump-back bridge ;

(*j*) where it will obscure a traffic sign ;

(*k*) near traffic lights ;

(*l*) near a pedestrian crossing.

66. Before opening any door of a vehicle, make sure that it will not endanger or inconvenience any other vehicle or anybody on the road or footpath. Get out on the nearside whenever possible.

The Highway Code
PART 3

THE ROAD USER AND ANIMALS

67. Keep your dog under control when you take it for a walk or in your car. Do not let your dog stray.

68. Make sure that the road is clear before you let or take an animal out on to the road.

69. If you are riding a horse, keep to the left.

70. When leading an animal in the road, always place yourself between it and the traffic, and keep the animal to the edge of the road.

71. If you are a drover and there is someone with you, send him on ahead to warn traffic at danger points such as bends and brows of hills. Carry lights after sunset.

The presence of dogs and other animals in the carriageway contributes to 4,000 accidents a year.

SIGNS AND
SIGNALS

1 **DRIVERS & RIDERS SIGNALS**
2 **POLICE SIGNALS**
3 **TRAFFIC SIGNS**
4 **TRAFFIC LIGHT SIGNALS**

Signs and signals are the language of the road. To ensure the safety of yourself and others, master this language.

1 DRIVERS AND RIDERS SIGNALS

The signals in this section should also be given by those in charge of horses.

"I am going to MOVE OUT or TURN to my RIGHT"

"I am going to TURN to my LEFT"

The left turn and right turn signals may also be given by a mechanical or flashing indicator.

SIGNA

Signal clearly, decisively and in good time. Fully extend
the arm. After signalling, do not carry out your intended
manœuvre until it is safe to do so.

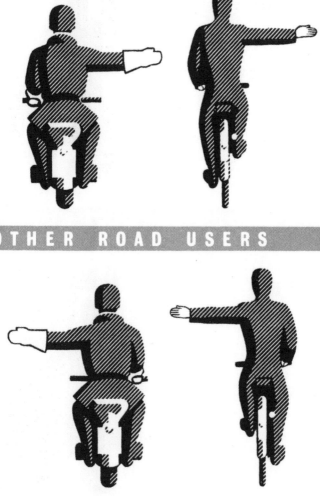

"I am ready to be OVERTAKEN"

This signal may also be used when pulling up at the kerb.
Drivers behind who want to overtake must make sure that it is safe to do so.

"I am going to SLOW DOWN or STOP"

This signal should be used also when slowing down or stopping at a zebra crossing.
It is NOT an invitation to overtake.

SIGNAL I

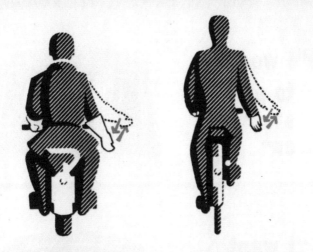

OOD TIME

"I want to go STRAIGHT ON"

"I want to turn LEFT"

"I want to turn RIGHT"

The left turn and right turn signals may also be given by a mechanical or flashing indicator.

MAKE TH

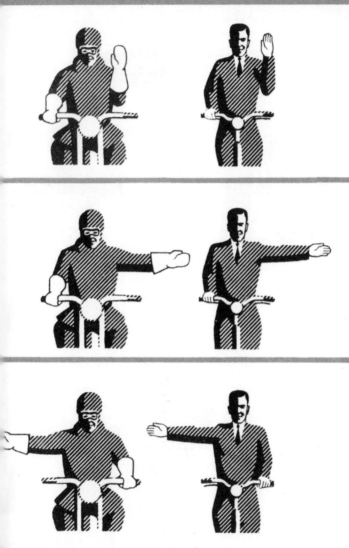

2 POLICE SIGNALS

STOP

STOP
Vehicle approaching
from front

STOP
Vehicle approaching
from behind

STOP
Vehicles
approaching
from both front
and behind

COME ON
Beckoning on a vehicle
from front

COME ON
Beckoning on a vehicle
from behind

COME ON
Beckoning on a vehicle
from the side

3 TRAFFIC SIGNS

Examples of **SIGNS WHICH MUST BE OBSERVED**

A red ring or a red disc is normally a feature of these signs.

SIGNS FOR APPROACHES TO MAJOR ROADS

Where a sign bears the word HALT the driver or rider of a vehicle must stop and wait until he is sure it is safe to go on.

SIGNS USED BY SCHOOL CROSSING PATROLS

Where a sign bears the word STOP the driver or rider must stop and wait for as long as the sign is displayed.

SIGNS WHICH SHOW PROHIBITION OR RESTRICTION ON THE USE OF ROADS

Speed Limit Begins.

Speed Limit Ends.
(These are Signs which Inform, see p. 25)

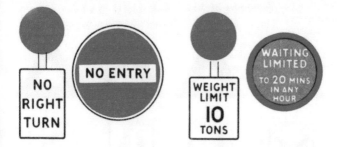

Posts for signs prohibiting or restricting waiting are normally striped with black and YELLOW bands.

ZEBRA CROSSINGS

On a Zebra Crossing, that is, a crossing marked by black and white stripes, studs and lighted beacons, pedestrians have the right of way unless a police officer is controlling traffic over it.

The double line of studs away from the crossing indicates the limit of the no-waiting area on the approach side of the crossing. On two-way roads these are found on both sides of the crossing ; on one-way roads the studs extend for the full width of the road on the approach side only. The studs do NOT indicate a reasonable stopping distance for an approaching vehicle.

Examples of **SIGNS WHICH WARN**

These signs are surmounted by a red triangle.

CROSS ROADS

ROAD JUNCTION

ROAD NARROWS

BEND

BENDS FOR 1¾ MILES

ROUND-ABOUT

LEVEL CROSSING

CROSSING NO GATES

HILL 1 IN 12

HUMP BRIDGE

LOW BRIDGE HEADROOM 14'-0"

SCHOOL

SAFETY POSTS AND DISCS
mark the edge of the carriageway or
obstructions near the edge.

NEARSIDE DISCS
have **red** reflectors
←

OFFSIDE DISCS
have **white** reflectors
→

24

Examples of SIGNS WHICH INFORM

These signs show where roads lead to, ends of
speed limits, parking places, etc.

APPROACH TO
ROAD JUNCTION

The road ahead is Route A 516.
The next place of any
importance in that direction is
Uttoxeter. This lies on Route A 50,
to which Route A 516 leads.

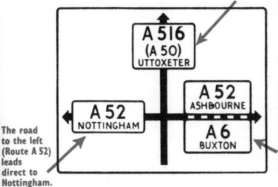

The road to the
right (Route A 52)
leads direct to
Ashbourne. The
chequer symbol
and the lower
panel show that
not far along
Route A 52 the
road joins
Route A 6 which
leads to Buxton.

The road
to the left
(Route A 52)
leads
direct to
Nottingham.

ROUTE SIGN

Placed just past a
road junction,
etc., so that
drivers may be
sure they have
taken the correct
route. Here
the route is A 16
and Route A 158
branches off not
far ahead.

OFFICIAL
CAR PARK SIGN

PLACE NAME
SIGN

Used in towns,
etc., to tell the
driver where
he is and the
mileage to the
next place of
importance.

HOSPITAL SIGN

NOTE. The signs in this Appendix are not all
drawn to the same scale.

25

4

TRAFFIC LIGHT SIGNALS

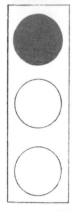

RED means STOP. Wait behind the stop line on the carriageway.

RED and AMBER also means STOP. Do not go until GREEN shows.

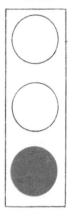

GREEN means you may GO ON if the road is clear. Take special care if you mean to turn left or right.

AMBER means STOP at the stop line. You may go on if the AMBER appears after you have crossed the stop line or are so close to it that to pull up might cause an accident.

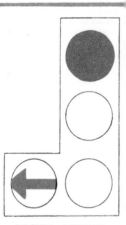

GREEN ARROW means that you may GO IN THE DIRECTION SHOWN BY THE ARROW. You may do this whatever other lights may be showing.

THE
LAW'S DEMANDS

Revised May, 1957

The following pages deal with major points of the law affecting safety on the roads. For the precise wording of the law you should refer to the various Acts and Regulations. These are indicated in the margin by the following abbreviations :

B.P.C.R. Brakes on Pedal Cycle Regulations, 1954.

C.U.R. Motor Vehicles (Construction and Use) Regulations, 1955.

D.L.A. Road Traffic (Driving Licences) Act, 1936.

D.L.R. Motor Vehicles (Driving Licences) Regulations, 1950.

H.A. Highway Act, 1835.

L.A. Licensing Act, 1872.

L.T.A. London Traffic Act, 1924.

P.C.R. Pedestrian Crossings Regulations, 1954.

R.T.A. Road Traffic Acts, 1930, 1934 and 1956.

R.T.L.A. Road Transport Lighting Acts, 1927–1953.

R.V.L.R. Road Vehicles Lighting Regulations, 1954–1955.

R.V.L. (Ex.) R. Road Vehicles Lighting (Standing Vehicles) (Exemption) Regulations, 1955 and 1956.

S.C.P.A. School Crossing Patrols Act, 1953.

V.S.L. Motor Vehicles (Variation of Speed Limit) Regulations, 1956.

P.C.R. No. 4   You have precedence when you are on the carriageway within the limits of an uncontrolled zebra crossing.

> NOTES (*a*) An uncontrolled zebra crossing is one at which traffic is not being controlled by a police officer and which is marked with two or more lighted beacons, black and white stripes, and studs to indicate the limits of the crossing.
>
> (*b*) You have NO precedence when you are standing on the kerb or when you are standing on a street refuge or central reservation which is on a zebra crossing.

YOU MUST NOT

P.C.R. No. 8   loiter on a pedestrian crossing ;

H.A. Sect. 72   wilfully cause obstruction of the footway or highway ;

R.T.A. 1956 Sect. 14   proceed along or across the carriageway when given a direction to stop by a police officer in uniform engaged in controlling traffic ;

R.T.A. 1930 Sect. 29   without lawful authority or reasonable cause, hold on to or get on a motor vehicle or trailer in motion or tamper with the brake or other part of the mechanism of a motor vehicle ;

L.A. Sect. 12   be drunk in any highway or public place.

TO PEDAL CYCLISTS

BEFORE CYCLING, make sure that

B.P.C.R. Nos. 3-5   your cycle has efficient brakes. (A bicycle must have an independent brake on each wheel except that if no wheel exceeds 18″ in diameter including tyre, only one brake is needed, and a fixed-wheel bicycle need have only one brake but that brake must operate on the front wheel. For tricycles see the Regulations.)

YOU MUST, EVEN IF YOU ARE WHEELING YOUR CYCLE,

R.T.A. 1930 Sect. 49   observe traffic signs and signals and the directions of a police officer controlling traffic ;

S.C.P.A. Sect. 2   stop when signalled to do so by a School Crossing Patrol ;

P.C.R. No. 4   give precedence to pedestrians on an uncontrolled zebra crossing, that is, a crossing marked by black and white stripes, studs and lighted beacons and at which there is no police officer controlling the traffic.

YOU MUST

R.T.L.A. 1927 Sects. 1 & 5, R.T.L.A. 1953 Sect. 1 and R.T.A. 1956 Sect. 41 — at night, see that your front and rear lamps are alight and that your cycle has an efficient red reflector ;

R.T.L.A. 1927 Sect. 5, and R.T.L.A. (Cycles) 1945 Sect. 3 — at night, if you are wheeling your cycle or are stationary without lights, keep as close as possible to the nearside edge of the road ;

R.T.A. 1956 Sect. 11(1) — stop when required to do so by a police officer in uniform.

YOU MUST NOT

P.C.R. No. 5 — stop your cycle within the limits of a pedestrian crossing, except in circumstances beyond your control or when it is necessary to do so to avoid an accident ;

R.T.A. 1956 Sect. 11(1) — ride recklessly or at a speed or in a manner which is dangerous to the public ;

,, — ride without due care and attention or without reasonable consideration for other persons using the road ;

,, — ride under the influence of drink or a drug ;

H.A. Sect. 72 — wilfully ride on a footpath by the side of any road made or set apart for the use of foot-passengers ;

H.A. Sect. 78 — by negligence or misbehaviour interrupt the free passage of any road user or vehicle ;

R.T.A. 1930 Sect. 50 — leave your cycle on any road in such a way that it is likely to cause danger to other road users ;

R.T.A. 1934 Sect. 20 — carry a passenger on a bicycle not constructed or adapted to carry more than one person ;

R.T.A. 1930 Sect. 29 — hold on to a motor vehicle or trailer in motion on any road.

TO DRIVERS OF MOTOR VEHICLES

BEFORE DRIVING, make sure that

R.T.A. 1930 Sect. 35 — your insurance is in order, i.e. that it covers the liabilities in respect of third party risks of yourself and any other person who may use your vehicle ;

R.T.A. 1930 Sect. 4, D.L.A. Sect. 3, D.L.R. No. 17 and R.T.A. 1956, Sect. 17 — you have a driving licence valid for the class of vehicle which you intend to drive, that it is not out of date, and that you have signed it in ink ;

R.T.A. 1930 Sect. 15 & R.T.A. 1956 Sect. 9 — you are not under the influence of drink or a drug ;

C.U.R. No. 73(1) — the condition of your vehicle and of any trailer it may be drawing and of all parts and accessories is such that no danger is likely to be caused to yourself or others ;

C.U.R. No. 76	your brakes and steering are in good working order and properly adjusted ;
C.U.R. No. 78	your tyres are free from defects likely to cause damage to the road or danger to yourself or others ;
C.U.R. Nos. 75 & 76	your windscreen is clean and the windscreen wiper in working order ;
C.U.R. No. 16	your vehicle has a mirror (two if it is not a private car) so fitted that you can see traffic behind you ;
C.U.R. No. 19	your horn is in working order ;
C.U.R. No. 74	your speedometer is in working order ;
C.U.R. No. 77(2)	your silencer is efficient ;
C.U.R. No. 81	your vehicle is not excessively noisy ;
C.U.R. No. 79	avoidable fumes and smoke are not emitted ;
C.U.R. No. 73	the load on your vehicle is not excessive or so badly distributed, packed or secured as to be dangerous ;
C.U.R. No. 102	your load if it overhangs sideways is not of illegal width ;
R.T.L.A. 1927-1953 and R.V.L.R.	your vehicle has lights and reflectors which comply with the regulations ;
R.V.L.R. Nos. 9 & 10	your headlights comply in particular with the anti-dazzle requirements.

When Driving

YOU MUST

C.U.R. No. 86	be in such a position that you can exercise proper control over your vehicle and retain a full view of the road and traffic ahead ;
P.C.R. No. 4	give precedence to a pedestrian who is on an uncontrolled zebra crossing, that is, a crossing marked by black and white stripes, studs and lighted beacons and at which there is no police officer controlling the traffic ;
R.T.A. 1930 Sect. 10 R.T.A. 1934 Sects. 1 & 2 and V.S.L. Schedule	observe speed limits in built-up areas or any speed limit to which your type of vehicle is subject ;
R.T.A. 1930 Sect. 49	observe traffic signs and signals and the directions of a police officer controlling traffic ;
R.T.A. 1930 Sect. 20(3)	stop when required to do so by a police officer in uniform ;
S.C.P.A. Sect 2	stop when signalled to do so by a School Crossing Patrol ;
R.T.L.A. 1927 Sect. 1 and R.T.A. 1956 Sect. 41	see that your side and tail lamps are alight at night.

YOU MUST NOT

R.T.A. 1930 Sect. 11	drive recklessly or at a speed or in a manner which is dangerous to the public ;
R.T.A. 1930 Sect. 12	drive without due care and attention or without reasonable consideration for other persons using the road ;
R.T.A. 1930 Sect. 15	drive under the influence of drink or a drug ;
C.U.R. No. 84	sound your horn at night (11.30 p.m.— 7 a.m.) in a built-up area.

When you stop

YOU MUST

C.U.R. No. 91	stop the engine and set the brake before you leave the vehicle ;
R.V.L.R. 1954 No. 13, R.T.L.A. 1927 Sect. 1, R.T.A. 1956 Sect. 41 and R.V.L. (Ex) R 1955 & 1956	switch off your headlights at night, but see that your side and tail lamps are alight ; on some roads governed by a speed limit, there are certain exemptions from showing side and tail lights when standing or parked in compliance with specified conditions.
R.T.A. 1930 Sects. 4 & 40	when required by the police, produce your driving licence and certificate of insurance for examination. If necessary, you may instead produce them within 5 days at any police station you select.

YOU MUST NOT

P.C.R. No. 6	stop your vehicle on the approach side of a pedestrian crossing beyond the double line of studs in the road (which are usually 15 yards from the crossing) except to give precedence to a pedestrian on the crossing, or in circumstances beyond your control, or when it is necessary to do so to avoid an accident;
P.C.R. No. 5	stop your vehicle within the limits of a crossing except in circumstances beyond your control or to avoid an accident;
C.U.R. No. 89	park your vehicle or trailer on the road so as to cause unnecessary obstruction;
R.T.A. 1930 Sect. 50	park your vehicle or trailer on the road in such a way that it is likely to cause danger to other road users;
C.U.R. No. 90	park at night on the " wrong " side of the road;
R.T.A. 1930 Sect. 46 and L.T.A. Sect. 10	park your vehicle in a " no-waiting " area or contrary to waiting restrictions;
C.U.R. No. 85	sound your horn while stationary.

R.T.A. 1930
Sects. 22 & 40
and R.T.A. 1956
8th Sched., Para. 15

which causes damage or injury to any other person, or other vehicle, or any animal (horse, cattle, ass, mule, sheep, pig, goat or dog) not in your vehicle

YOU MUST

(*a*) stop ;

(*b*) give your own and the vehicle owner's name and address and the registration mark of the vehicle to anyone having reasonable grounds for requiring them ;

(*c*) if you do not give your name and address to any such person at the time, report the accident to the police as soon as reasonably practicable, and in any case within 24 hours ;

(*d*) if anyone is injured and you do not produce your certificate of insurance at the time to the police or to anyone who has with reasonable grounds required its production, report the accident to the police as soon as possible, and in any case within 24 hours, and produce your certificate of insurance to the police, either when reporting the accident or within 5 days thereafter at any police station you select.

TO MOTOR CYCLISTS and RIDERS of MOTOR-ASSISTED PEDAL CYCLES

Most of the requirements of the law relating to motor drivers, including those relating to pedestrian crossings, apply to you. In addition :

YOU MUST NOT

R.T.A. 1930
Sect. 16 and
C.U.R. No. 101

carry more than one passenger on a two-wheeled machine, and the passenger must sit astride the cycle on a proper seat securely fitted behind the driver's seat and with proper rests for the feet.

When visiting the countryside PLEASE REMEMBER

Guard against all risk of fire	Leave no litter
Fasten all gates	Safeguard water supplies
Keep dogs under proper control	Protect wild life, wild plants, and trees
Keep to paths across farm land	
Avoid damaging fences, hedges and walls	Go carefully on country roads
	Respect the life of the countryside

From " THE COUNTRY CODE" booklet, drawn up by the National Parks Commission and published by Her Majesty's Stationery Office. Price 4d. net.